Believing Makes Sense

Believing Makes Sense

A way of reading the Bible

Lucas Grollenberg

SCM PRESS LTD

Translated by John Bowden from the Dutch
Geloven is zo gek nog niet,
published by Uitgeverij Ten Have n.v., Baarn.

© Uitgeverij Ten Have 1983

English translation © John Bowden 1983

334 00096 3

First published 1983 by
SCM Press Ltd
26-30 Tottenham Road London N1

Printed in Great Britain by
Richard Clay (The Chaucer Press) Ltd
Bungay, Suffolk

Contents

Preface

In recent years I have often been invited to discuss texts from the Bible with all kinds of people, in groups of various sizes. On a number of occasions I've been asked to put the substance of our discussion down on paper. The present book is an attempt to do that. It describes how on different occasions I have discussed themes and texts from the Bible. What my accounts of these meetings have in common is that I always begin from the question what the biblical writers meant by their texts in their own time; that's called a 'historical approach'. Many people approach the Bible differently, and I sometimes hear that the historical approach is thought to be out of date. However, it seems to me to be indispensable for Christians who want to retain the possibility of discussing their belief honestly, not only among themselves but also with outsiders, to whom it seems nonsense. To be honest, I originally intended a more systematic discussion of Christian belief and the possibility of communicating. However, as I wrote, I felt happier discussing the texts and their background.

Lucas Grollenberg

1   Common Sense about the Bible

I had been invited to spend three evenings talking on the question 'What can the Bible mean in our life?' On the first evening I had hardly said anything before someone anxiously asked about 'the message'. 'Good grief,' I thought, 'you can't get on to the subject of the Bible without the question of a message immediately coming up.' I politely replied that we would certainly get to the message in due course, but that first we should look and see what the Bible really is.

About seventy people had enrolled for these evenings, in Best, near Eindhoven. They were a very mixed bunch: Catholics and Protestants, men and women of all ages and backgrounds. So I began by saying that the word 'Bible' would conjure up different ideas in each of us, between the two extremes of vague memories from our youth and detailed knowledge; and that for each of us these memories would be associated with very different images and feelings. 'If you are going to talk to one another about the meaning that the Bible can have in your life,' I went on, 'you must agree on a particular, well-defined picture of the book, something that comes before all theories and can be demonstrated and made plausible to anybody. In other words, you must agree about what the Bible obviously is, otherwise you are just talking at cross-purposes, and that kind of discussion doesn't make much sense.' So I did what I often do on such occasions. First, I remind people of the 'books' which make up the Old Testament. Then I draw on a blackboard or large sheet of paper a time chart from 1200 BC to AD 100. On it I draw the great periods of history, from Moses through David and the kings of Israel and Judah to the period of Judaism. Then I indicate at what point on this chart, i.e. in what period, particular parts of the Old Testament came into being; after that, I go on to show how these pieces finally came together into one book. Because I get so involved, the chairman usually has to tell me that it's time for a break, because when I get so caught up in the history of our faith I never find that I have enough time.

That's what happened in Best. After the break, it emerged that many people were astonished. For instance, I had demonstrated that Jewish faith was expressed clearly for the first time when the people of Judah were living in exile in Babylon, round about 550 BC. Only then did they realize that their national God had no other gods beside him, and therefore had to be the creator and ruler of everything that existed and would exist. During the exile the sabbath took on the special significance that it was to have among the Jews all down the centuries. This meant, for example, that the chapter with which the Bible begins, describing how God created the world in six days and rested on the seventh, cannot have been written before the exile. Only then, too, could the conviction arise that through the bond that tied them to the one God, the Jews were 'chosen' from among all peoples to be witnesses to his reality.

On the second evening I did the same thing with the New Testament. First I recalled the twenty-seven 'books', some of them no more than booklets, even pamphlets, which make up that part of the Bible. Then I went back to the blackboard. In the top left-hand corner I put the date 30 and at the bottom 130. In the middle at the top I put a cross: that represented the brief career of Jesus, which I like to describe as 'an explosion of humanity'.

Underneath, over the course of this century, I filled in the times when the best-known writings of the New Testament were composed. First came some letters by Paul, and rather lower, after the year 70, the four Gospels.

This scheme, too, surprised some people. They were surprised, for example, by the fact that Paul had already been preaching 'the gospel' for thirty years, and on that basis had founded Christian communities in many cities round about the eastern Mediterranean, by the time the first Gospel, that of Mark, was written.

So the blackboard showed the interval between Jesus and the four Gospels. The reminiscences which these books contained were first handed down for dozens of years by word of mouth in Christian groups made up of very different people. Among other things, this means that there are always at least three elements in each one of the small units (scholars call them pericopes) of which the Gospels are formed: first a recollection of the earthly life of Jesus, what he said or did or had done to him; then all kinds of indications of the way in which the believers who handed down the stories by word of mouth of course 'coloured' them in the light of their own situation; and finally the traces of the author, the evangelist, who handed down a particular part of the tradition in his own style and included it in one place rather than another in his work. I then gave a few examples to illustrate how much richer a text from the Gospels can become when you listen to it as it were in 'stereo'.

Although I felt that the historical surveys on these two evenings were far too brief, they did make it clear to all those who were present that the Bible grew in a process which took more than ten centuries, and that hundreds, many hundreds of writers and copyists were involved in that process. On the third evening, on the basis of this understanding we had now all arrived at, we could deal with a number of questions about our beliefs. I introduced the discussion with a few thoughts. First, I pointed out that no one in earlier times had been able to do what we had done. What I meant was that no one had been able to visualize the Bible as having 'grown' by a gradual process. Since the nineteenth century we Westerners have learned to think in terms of developments, of processes. I had just been reading a book by an English biologist entitled *Creation and the World of Science*. According to the author, in the last twenty years the various branches of natural sciences have increasingly arrived at a unanimous view of the origin of the earth and the universe, of which we human beings are a part. Millions and millions of years ago, a dense nucleus exploded. This explosion produced the stellar systems, finally including the one to which our solar system belongs; of this our earth is one of the smaller planets. An atmospheric ring formed around this earth, making life possible. Within it, organisms developed, of increasing refinement, each one better equipped to survive in the constantly changing environment. So after many millions of years, the species to which we belong came into being. Our species does

3

not just react to stimuli from outside; we ourselves can change the environment on the basis of our self-awareness. This awareness enables us to say 'I', and to say 'you' to others of the same species, thus bringing about a completely new form of society which we call human culture. When you look at this development, this English scholar wrote, and realize how we human beings have emerged from the stuff of the universe, you feel bewildered and amazed.

He had written his book to argue that with such a vision of the world we must understand belief in God as 'creator of heaven and earth' in different terms from those common in earlier Christian teaching. However, I didn't go into that point. I wanted to arrive at a specific question. We can see that the Bible came into being in a process which took centuries – something else to reduce you to silence if you really look at it closely – but that process has come to an end. The end came somewhere in the third century of our era. At that time the text of the Bible was finally established. No more additions, no extra material. The Bible now is precisely what it was then. You could say that it has become petrified.

All other areas of human society, of 'culture', have undergone developments. Christian Europe came into being, and at one stage was almost overwhelmed by the higher culture of Islam. Later, hitherto unknown parts of the earth were discovered; there were revolutionary developments in science, in technology, in patterns of society, and so on. All this has made us different from the people who wrote the Bible.

Modern forms of communication have also deeply influenced our feeling about life. When astronauts circled the moon for the first time, they sent back television pictures in which you could see the earth, a bluish sphere like a jewel, shining against the infinite blackness of space. Photographs of it appeared in newspapers throughout the world, so the majority of people have seen them. This picture has now become part of us. It arouses feelings of wonderment, but it reminds us of our smallness, our nothingness. It also makes us realize how vulnerable we really are. I recall a poster with this splendid photograph of the earth and under it the slogan, 'Look after your local planet!' The several thousand million of us can only go on living in that thin atmospheric layer if we look after it very carefully. And what is

4

disturbing an increasing number of people is that we aren't really doing that. The great powers have developed weapons which can make large parts of the earth uninhabitable in a flash. Were that to happen, the living would envy the dead. And alongside that there are lesser powers who fight amongst one another and kill thousands of people each week, while elsewhere in the world countless of our fellow human beings die of starvation as a consequence of our Western arrogance and greed.

That is how I led up to the question that we were to discuss on the last evening, the question of 'the message' of the Bible. How can this book, written so long ago, by people who lived in such a different world, much more 'primitive' than ours, still speak to us, help us to look for an answer to our questions about the meaning of the universe, and above all teach us to go through this terrifying world with some hope?

The discussion was opened by someone who was obviously disturbed. I had never at any point said that the Bible comes from God, that it is 'God's word', and if you lose sight of that, of course you have problems! 'In your view,' I was told, 'the Bible is just an ordinary human book!' After the previous evenings I could point out in my answer that the Bible is not at all an ordinary book, and is quite unique in our culture simply by virtue of the way in which it was written. An ordinary book is usually written by one man or woman. Sometimes a number of authors collaborate in particular books, as with collections of essays on a particular subject, or composite works like encyclopaedias. But a book in which hundreds of authors have been involved over a period of more than ten centuries cannot be compared with any other book.

Moreover, ordinary books deal with specific subjects, and fall into particular recognizable categories. A travel account differs from a collection of poems, and a novel can easily be distinguished from a history book. An encyclopaedia deals with everything you can think of and more, but only from the point of view of providing information; you won't find poems, challenges or short stories in it.

The Bible contains an enormous amount of literature, all jumbled together; an amazing number of stories, short and long, of very different kinds; sometimes they seem to recount history and sometimes they are obviously meant above all to express feelings and ideas and to be provocative. There are also poems and prayers, cries from the heart and love songs; visions, sermons, sometimes encouraging, often threatening and condemning. There are also a great many regulations about sacrifice, genealogies, discussions about good and evil, and so on. The Bible is really a whole library in one volume.

So the Bible is not an ordinary book. But it is human through and through. That is because it is about everything that can happen to people from birth to death; it is about their lives as families and as nations; it is about love and happiness, quarrelling and hatred, treachery, murder and war, about the agony of individuals and peoples. Some writers recall the past, how their people began, and even how mankind began; others give visions of the future. Dozens of great figures emerge, successful and gifted people, kings and prophets, and also some women, to all of whom nothing human is alien; then finally there is the figure of Jesus, so completely human that he is greeted as the beginning of a new humanity. What holds all this together is faith in the one God who is involved in everything. It was precisely that explicit belief which all these people had in common and which made it possible for so many and such different writings from their circle finally to grow together to form the one book, the book of this community of the faith.

Within this community, first in its Jewish phase and later in its Christian phase, the writings were preserved, used and constantly recopied, because they were so to speak the documentation for the belief in God which kept everybody together. In this way, what people of former generations had experienced in their life as marked with their relationship with God were recorded and preserved, and could be recalled, time and time again. Believers saw this, too, as a gracious act of God. He too had used the means by which people share and record everything among themselves, the written word, in order as it were to guarantee his faithfulness. Judaism expressed its esteem for these 'holy' scriptures, especially the Torah, in all kinds of ways. For example, they said that Moses was the author of that book. But this man, the greatest of all their prophets, had not written the work himself; no, God had inspired him with it all, had prompted him, and this text was already with God before he created the world.

When a number of Jews began to see the crucified Jesus of Nazareth as the expected Messiah and the Son of God, the beginning of the 'fulfilment' of the whole relationship that had previously been experienced between God and man, all the words of God in this holy book seemed to them to point towards this fulfilment. Later they added writings by members of their own group to this holy book of the Jews, and the whole work became the Christian 'Bible' (the Greek word for book). In order to express their reverence for this book, the Christians took over a number of images and expressions from Jews. For instance, they said that the authors of the Bible were 'inspired'; in other words, God had breathed into them what they put down on paper; moreover, the author of the whole book is God himself, so the Bible is 'God's word', and so on.

I used terms like esteeming and revering. It was the community of believers who regarded this particular book, with all the different writings in it, as a gift from their God, a written account of his earlier dealings with his people and thus a documentation of his faithfulness, a kind of written guarantee of his plans: 'This is how I shall always deal with you.' You might say it was a last will and testament, but that term is less appropriate, since in our language it presupposes someone's death, whereas God is the living one. What I want to say here is that the book has this special character only in the eyes of believers.

When this was clear to those present we could join together in exploring all kinds of questions, like the one about 'the message'. Perhaps we do not need to be active members of a church community, but belief in the 'personal' God of the biblical tradition seems necessary if we are to be tuned in to the wavelength of those whose words we hear in the Bible, if we are to be able to receive their 'message'. Without that belief, certain parts of the Bible may speak to us as literature, even great literature, which does not leave the reader untouched – but that is something different from perceiving in it a word from the God with whom people feel a bond, in whose presence they go through life. Only in this way, it seems, by virtue of that faith, can the old texts – I said earlier that they were 'petrified' – begin to speak to us again. And when that happens, these people from a much earlier age, whose words we hear in them, in a sense become our contemporaries.

But is it possible for people of our time to have such a biblical sense of a 'personal' God who is involved in everything and also with us? Can we have that sense which was so alive among these earlier people, which permeated their way of life together and their view of everything, their expectations and their hope? Can we modern men and women, who live in a world without God, cultivate such a sense? Do we perhaps have to be programmed for it by our upbringing? Or is faith something just a matter of disposition, like being musical – either you have it or you don't? Can you practise faith, and if so, how? Can you communicate it to others, and if so, in what way?

People went home asking themselves this kind of question on that last evening, and I was satisfied with that. In my view it is much better to live with real questions than with answers given too readily. Since it had been a tiring evening, I was glad that someone had left a newspaper behind in the late train. The headlines and the pictures distracted me a bit. But one report brought me back again to the subject of the evening. It was about plans to devote a whole year to the 'evangelization' of our country. I have an antipathy to the term 'evangelize'. It not only makes me think of instant conversions on a large scale, but also conjures up a picture of someone knocking on the door and disturbing people without first having made any real human contact.

I have the same sort of resistance towards the way in which Bibles are distributed too widely and too soon, are even just thrust on people, clearly in the hope that 'the word of God' will have its effect. But the Bible received that name within the community of faith. Before printing was invented, copying Bibles by hand, transcribing them, was a religious matter; you became involved in it so that the documentation of God's faithfulness would be handed down to subsequent generations of the family of believers. So we might really best call the Bible a 'family book', strange and confusing to anyone unfamiliar with the traditions of this family. Since Bibles have been printed, it has been possible to sell them and distribute them without making any contact with a believing comunity. And that is what has happened, above all since the last century. Every year millions and millions of them are still published for this kind of distribution. But what is the purpose of it? I recall an article in a Bible

8

society journal with the headline, 'The best-seller without read-ers'. Of course it can happen that someone in loneliness and despair picks up a Bible and then is suddenly moved by a passage which opens up a new perspective. But that seems to me to be exceptional. Bibles which are forced on people remain unread. The best kind of propaganda still seems to me to be a pattern of human life and society which is convincing and attractive, and which so amazes and attracts outsiders that they ask the question 'What's behind all this?' In that case the Bible will also come up as part of the answer.

Perhaps my objection to all kinds of 'evangelization' is rooted in my intellectual approach to a whole variety of things. I must have given this impression of being an intellectual to one of those present on that last evening in Best. During the break, a woman came up to me and asked, 'Do *you* really believe?' I was completely flabbergasted! How could someone come up so abruptly and ask one of the most intimate questions possible? When I asked, 'What do you mean?', she replied, 'Well, you know a great deal and you talk so easily about it, so I thought to myself, "Does he really believe?"' Before I could give her an answer, she came to the real reason why she had asked; her husband had died, quite unexpectedly. That had shattered her faith. It seemed as if there was nothing left. She could no longer pray as she used to.

There was hardly time for a conversation. I said the first thing that occurred to me. I mentioned psalmists complaining to God in their distress, 'Why have you left me in the lurch?' I mentioned the person who said to Jesus, 'Lord, help my unbelief!' And I quoted a remark by Etty Hillesum. The diary of this Jewish woman, covering the years 1941-1943, was published in Holland in 1981 and has continued to make a strong impression on many Christians (it was published in English in 1983 under the title *Etty: A Diary*). Etty had come to live in Amsterdam in 1932 as an eighteen-year-old law student. After finishing that course, she went on to study Russian language and literature. Later in this book, in chapter 10, I shall be describing how she found the courage to kneel down and to address God. That was in the early spring of 1941, just before she started writing a diary. With an amazing frankness she describes what made up her daily life, including the increasingly painful and threatening measures taken by the Germans against the Jews, soon resulting in mass deportations. Another element is made up of Etty's relationships with other Jewish people, particularly Julius Spier, her much older friend, and her conversations with God. She speaks to him in her own vocabulary and style, with no trace of traditional formulas. From her many reflections on human life and destiny it appears that she has made herself familiar with Russian authors like Dostoievsky and Tolstoy, with the German poet Rilke, with the *Confessions* of St Augustine and also with parts of the Bible, Old and New Testaments. In August 1942 she went to Westerbork, the 'transit' camp for her fellow Jews waiting there to be transported to 'the East', to do social work among them. She managed to keep on writing, in the most unlikely times and places in the camp. She sent many letters to her family and friends, some of which have recently been published in Dutch under the title 'The Thinking Heart of the Barracks'. They give a vivid impression of the unspeakable distress of the deported Jews, their old and sick people and their new born babies, expecting every day to be driven into a goods van. At the same time these letters reflect Etty's attitude, revealing profound inner peace and showing an unflagging power to love. On 7 September 1943, she and her family were transported. A few days later, farmers found a postcard by the railway line, which Etty had managed to throw out. It contains a few lines addressed to her friend Christine. The first line contains a short exclamation of confidence, quoted from the Psalms as rendered in the 1637 *Statenbijbel*, the Dutch equivalent of the 1611 Authorized/King James Version. The seventeenth-century Dutch of the quotation could be rendered, 'The Lord is my high chamber', in modern translations '...my high refuge, my stronghold or my fortress'. The line is followed by some information about her departure and greetings to friends.

I have mentioned this because it illustrates for me what I was trying to say about the Bible as providing a sort of basic 'vocabulary' of faith, used by the 'family' of believers throughout the centuries.

2 The Old Testament Chart: The Origin of the First Part of the Bible

The people in Best asked me to put down everything on paper, especially the time charts from the two previous evenings. I didn't dare promise anything. Charts like those on the board 'grow' in the course of an evening. While I was drawing lines and arrows and filling in names, I was talking all the time. And the same thing went on during the discussion: I added things when remarks or questions called for it. Those present saw the board getting fuller, with periods and names which were important. It was an exercise in communication, which cannot really be put down in writing. What I can do, though, is to give you the bare bones of the chart, together with a certain amount of information, and leave it to you to fill in the details for yourselves.

The chart on page 13 has a time-scale running from top to bottom, from 1200 BC to about AD 100. After the names at the top there's quite a gap. The political history of which we have any knowledge only begins with David and Solomon. The two columns under their names indicate the two parts of the kingdom of Israel which became independent after the death of King Solomon. Alongside the arrows, on the left you can see the name Assyria and on the right Egypt, because Palestine formed the main line of communication between these two great cultural areas. David and Solomon were able to establish and maintain their kingdom because in their time there was no power of any significance either to the north or to the south. Things began to change in the period after 900, when the Assyrians emerged. In their effort to establish their rule over Egypt via Palestine, in 721 they annihilated the kingdom of Israel. They deported the remnants of the civil population to other parts of their realm and settled colonists in their place. Thus that kingdom permanently vanished from the scene as a political entity. Shortly after that the Assyrians launched an attack on the much smaller kingdom of Judah in the south, but fell short of conquering it. Evidently they thought it important to have control of a completely dependent vassal state on this southernmost point of their route to Egypt.

Thinking people in Judah must have asked themselves what Israel had done to deserve this terrible fate. That was clear to a number of them: the inhabitants of the northern kingdom had worshipped many other gods and goddesses; some of them they had inherited from the Canaanites already living there, and some were native gods brought by outsiders who had settled in Israel, especially people at the court. That had to be the reason why they had been punished with complete annihilation by the Assyrians. So it was also clear that if the people of Judah wanted to go on existing, they had to put aside all this 'idolatry' and worship only their own national God, Yahweh.

The king of Jerusalem, along with the priests of his temple, may well have wanted something like this, but it was extremely difficult for their subjects, certainly in the provinces. The local sanctuaries and all that went on in them were very much a part of daily life. It was easy for people to talk about their ideal of 'Yahweh alone', especially when it became clear what their talk also, of course, implied: all the sacrifices and all the festivities which went with a sacrifice could only take place in the temple in Jerusalem. The state, the king and the priests had an economic interest in it.

Alongside the column for Judah, at about the year 640, we find the name Josiah on the time scale. He was a king who tried to carry through the exclusive worship of Yahweh. In his time Assyrian pressure was on the decline and Egypt was becoming stronger. That aroused the hope of independence at the court and - who knows? – perhaps even hope of the restoration of the kingdom of David to its former size. This was one more reason for purifying the worship of the national God of all Canaanite and foreign influences. Josiah organized a large-scale 'reform',

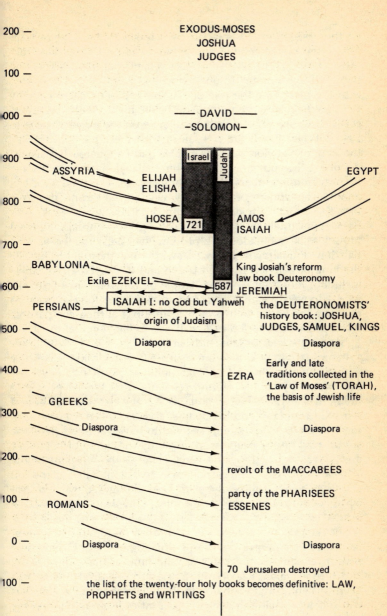

200 —

EXODUS-MOSES
JOSHUA
JUDGES

100 —

000 — ——— DAVID ———
–SOLOMON–

900 —

ASSYRIA

Israel | Judah

ELIJAH
ELISHA

EGYPT

800 —

HOSEA   721   AMOS
ISAIAH

700 —

BABYLONIA

King Josiah's reform
law book Deuteronomy

Exile EZEKIEL   587

600 —   JEREMIAH

PERSIANS   ISAIAH I: no God but Yahweh   the DEUTERONOMISTS'
history book: JOSHUA,
JUDGES, SAMUEL, KINGS

origin of Judaism

500 —

Diaspora   Diaspora

400 —   EZRA   Early and late
traditions collected in the
'Law of Moses' (TORAH),
the basis of Jewish life

GREEKS

300 —

Diaspora   Diaspora

200 —   revolt of the MACCABEES

100 —   party of the PHARISEES
ESSENES
ROMANS

0 —

Diaspora   Diaspora

70 Jerusalem destroyed

100 —   the list of the twenty-four holy books becomes definitive: LAW,
PROPHETS and WRITINGS

13

on the basis of an old law book which emerged during restoration work in the temple and which was said to derive from Moses. Perhaps it has been preserved in chapters 12-20 of the book of Deuteronomy in our Bible.

In the meantime the role of Assyria had been taken over by the new Babylonian empire. The Babylonians, too, were interested in having an obedient small state on the military route to Egypt. When Judah did not fall in with these plans, in 597 BC the king of Babylon sent his armies and conquered Jerusalem, deporting the young king Jehoiachin to Babylon along with some thousands of members of the ruling classes. The conqueror put another descendant of the royal house on the throne and gave him the name Zedekiah, expecting that he would look after Babylonian interests. But this weak figure eventually allowed himself to be persuaded by a pro-Egyptian party to rebel against Babylon. Punishment followed swiftly and thoroughly; in 587 the king of Babylon invaded Judah and destroyed all its cities, including Jerusalem and the temple of Yahweh. Those citizens who survived the massacre had to make the long journey to Babylon and began to live there with those of their compatriots who had been deported earlier. It was in Babylon that the foundations were laid for later Judaism.

In any age, to be driven out by force of arms from the country where you have lived for generations is a terrible fate. At the same time, it was a profound religious crisis for the people of Judah in Babylon. Their national God Yahweh, who had bound himself to his land and his people, and had taken up his abode in the temple of Jerusalem, seemed to have vanished from the scene. Had he too been swept away by the might of Babylon's gods? Was he in the same sorry state as the remnant of the Judaeans who had been carried away to distant Babylon and felt that they were completely lost? They thought they were finished, with no existence as a people, really dead and without a future.

Thanks to some individuals with deep faith and inspiration, Jewish belief emerged out of this situation of crisis. On the time scale two names appear against the time of the exile, Ezekiel and Second Isaiah. Ezekiel was a priest from Jerusalem who had been carried away to Babylon in the deportation of 597. He was led to believe that Yahweh was present even there, among the

14

remnant of his people in that distant heathen land, and that he would continue with them once they recognized their guilt and made an honest choice for him and only for him.

The other name, Second Isaiah, denotes the man whose sayings have been written down in chapters 40 to 55 of the biblical book of Isaiah. This inspired figure put into words things that no one had said so clearly before him: Yahweh is the only God, so there are no other gods beside him. Whereas all the peoples of the world at that time imagined that the divine world consisted of families of gods in which fathers and mothers, gods and goddesses, produced offspring, they heard Yahweh say: 'No god was formed before me and there shall be none after me. I am the first and the last, and apart from me there is no god.' Therefore the origin of all things can lie only with Yahweh. He is the one who has made everything, 'heaven and earth'. But in that case he also has all that exists in his hands. And in that case he has world history under control, so that the Judaeans in Babylonia need not be anxious about their future: 'Yahweh can and Yahweh will be their saviour and redeemer.'

Alongside these two great figures there were doubtless others who also gave direction to the community of exiles from Judah. In this way a special group began to take shape increasingly clearly in the midst of peoples who took for granted a multiplicity of gods. Over these years customs and practices came into being which clearly expressed the sense of being separate; in other words, they made this separateness in religion clear both to the people from Judah and to the world outside.

Think, for example, of circumcision. This was a practice customary among the inhabitants of ancient Canaan and the countries around, and also among the Egyptians, but it was unusual in Babylon. Thus the fact that the Jews were circumcised became a sign that they formed a group, were worshippers of Yahweh, and in this way became a sign of the covenant. It was then laid down that every male child had to be circumcised on the eighth day after his birth as a new member of the people who stood apart because they recognized no other God than Yahweh and put their trust in him alone.

The rules of 'purity' gradually became very important. In ancient Israel, as among other agrarian peoples, there had been certain taboos; for example, people were forbidden to eat the

15

flesh of some animals. In the exile some of these taboos were developed into binding rules for the whole community, again as a means of expressing their consecration to the one God. Another word for this consecration is holiness: in all that they did and experienced the Judaeans had to express the fact that they were the people of the one God, 'a holy people, a priestly nation'.

In Babylon we also find the beginnings of what later was to become 'holy scripture'. A move in this direction had already been made by people working at the time of King Josiah, whom I mentioned earlier in connection with a revival of nationalism which accompanied a religious reformation. These people, whom we call the 'Deuteronomists', after the law book that was found, assembled all kinds of documentary material from the nation's past, literature that was both written and handed down by word of mouth. There was material about Joshua, who conquered the land; about the judges, Samuel and the first king, Saul; about David and Solomon and the kings of Israel and Judah; and about prophets who appeared in their reigns. They gathered all this documentation together into a great history work, which had a clear message and so was a kind of sermon at the same time. In effect, what it said was this: if the nation falls away from Yahweh by worshipping other gods, it will be punished with disasters, and now that his temple has been established in Jerusalem the same is true of those who offer sacrifices to him in other places.

In our Bible this great work is spread over four books: Joshua, Judges, Samuel and Kings. We can see from the last book that it was completed only at the time of the exile, when the fall of Jerusalem had painfully confirmed the message of the work as a whole.

At the same time, the priests in particular among the deported Judaeans were busy collecting, arranging and above all supplementing stories about Moses and the Exodus, and sagas about the patriarchs of Israel long before. Earlier, in Jerusalem, they had already come across old myths about the creation of the world, the gods and men, which circulated in Canaan, and they could develop this knowledge still further in the vicinity of the holy city of Babylon. They incorporated elements of them into stories which they made for their own people, characterized by

16

their belief in Yahweh as the only God, creator of all things, stories in which they could also express their skill in the use of numbers and their interest in genealogies.

But now, back to the time chart. About the level of the sixth century you can see an arrow coming in from the left with the name 'Persians' by it. This non-Semitic people from the east put an end to the power of Babylon in 539 by seizing their capital. The Persians gave the peoples who had been deported freedom to return to their homeland. Cyrus, the king of Persia, was influenced by a religious approach which sought to recognize only one God. So he could feel sympathy for the Judaeans, who had arrived at a similar belief. From 538, groups of them took the opportunity to return to Jerusalem. There in 520 they began to rebuild the temple, with financial support from the Persians.

All this laid the foundation for Judaism. In Aramaic, which was the vernacular of the time, the name Judaeans, citizens of the kingdom of Judah, was pronounced *yehudai*. In Greek, which has no letter *h*, after the addition of the usual ending for a masculine noun, *os*, this word became *iudaios*. Our word Jew is derived from that.

Alongside 'origin of Judaism' on the chart you will see the word 'Diaspora'. This is the usual (Greek) term for the 'dispersion' of the Jews over the world of the time. After 538, many of the Jews did not go back with those returning home; they remained in Babylon, and families from there later began to settle elsewhere in the East. Even before the disaster of 587, families from Judah had already migrated to Egypt in order to make a new life there.

Round about the year 400 you will see the name Ezra, who is known as the 'father of Judaism'. This scribe had connections with the Persian court and used his position to make 'the book of the law of Yahweh' the basis of Jewish life. Hence his title.

'Greeks' stands alongside the next arrow from the left. With Alexander the Great they began to dominate the political scene. His successors in Egypt had a great struggle with those in Syria over the possession of Palestine. That was a good reason for many Jews to get out of the way and settle in the many newly-built cities in Asia and around the Mediterranean.

In the second century the Maccabaean revolt was important for Jewish life in Palestine. The Maccabaeans fought for the right of the Jews to live in accordance with the precepts of the Torah. The enemy was a powerful ruler from Syria who wanted to force an identical way of life on all his subjects. However, the successors of the Maccabees were very worldly, pagan princes, and that became the occasion for believing Jews to begin to form special groups like the Essenes, and above all the Pharisees.

The last arrow from the left has the name 'Romans' beside it. From the year 63 BC they ruled Palestine. This constantly led to popular revolts, which became increasingly violent. In the end, in AD 70 Jerusalem and the temple were destroyed. After that, the leaders of the only surviving group, the Pharisees, succeeded in keeping the Jewish community from falling apart by giving it a new centre, the Torah, to replace Jerusalem and the temple. In this reorganization it was also necessary to establish which writings belonged to the 'Holy Books'. Here the extent of the Hebrew Old Testament was settled once and for all.

Biblical history writing

Do ordinary readers of the Bible need to know all this? Not in detail, but I do think that they should have some awareness of it. Let me mention two insights which are of great importance if we are not to misunderstand the stories in the Bible. The first is the tremendous difference in the forms of the stories. The history work of the 'Deuteronomists', in our Bible spread over the books from Joshua up to and including Kings, contains a whole range of forms: popular stories about legendary heroes from far back in the past, like Samson, or recent popular figures, like David; legends about prophets like Elijah and Elisha; passages from official documents like the court chronicles with the years of the reigns and the public actions of the kings of Israel and Judah; a great deal of authentic literature about the history of king David and his sons, in which the brilliant writer has made the most of his proximity to the events; stories with a moral intent, for instance those in which the Deuteronomists make great figures like Joshua and Samuel deliver speeches addressed to the readers of their history work.

In Genesis and in the later books of the Torah there is an even greater difference. Genesis first introduces stories about creation, paradise, the flood and the tower of Babel which are of a very special kind. The Jewish writers incorporated many elements which they knew from all kinds of ancient Near Eastern myths. It is probably best to call the following stories about Abraham and his sons 'sagas', tales about patriarchs which were handed down and retold over the centuries and which in the process came to include as well the repeatedly new experiences of later generations.

Originally only a few reminiscences were in circulation about Moses, the Exodus from Egypt and the stay in the wilderness, among small groups of tribes which were to form the people Israel. In these recollections the figure of Moses was understood as the man to whom God had made himself known as Yahweh, saviour and deliverer of the group of Hebrews who as a result felt a permanent bond with him. Hence over the course of centuries all kinds of stories with all kinds of meanings were constantly added to the account of this 'foundation' period. So too were collections of laws and regulations which had been made and observed in later periods of Israel's history. These regulations were supposed already to have been promulgated by God in the wilderness period with Moses as his spokesman. Hence the extent and the richness of the four other books of the Torah, from Exodus to Deuteronomy.

Here we come to a second characteristic of biblical history writing. In a great many stories which give us the impression of presenting history, past and present are in fact blended together. In other words, the part of the past about which the story is told is as it were clothed, filled out, with all kinds of data from a later period, mostly things which were important in the world of the narrator.

Let me give one example from the many which occur to me. In the book of Exodus there are thirteen chapters, 25-31 and 35-40, which most readers skip over. They describe how God wanted the portable sanctuary in the wilderness, the 'tabernacle', to be built and equipped; they then go on to describe in just as much detail how the Israelites carried out all these instructions. There is no doubt that these passages were written by Jewish priests during and after the exile. In doing so they worked over earlier information – and for example they had in mind the measurements and the arrangements of the temple of Solomon (which by then had been destroyed). But their design was that portable structure as a whole. One might say that this was a kind of confession of faith put into practice, or perhaps better, an ideal, a utopia; here the priests tried to give expression to their faith, the conviction contained here: the God who willed to dwell in the midst of his people and to remain with them no matter what happened had to be served with all this dedication and care.

You can go and gape at an accurate 'reconstruction' of this wilderness sanctuary in the Biblical Museum in Amsterdam. If you do, it is worth remembering that it represents an ideal formed in the minds of these priests which existed only on paper, as the expression of a living faith in the God who is completely other: holy, yet at the same time very close. So the practical question where those who built this tabernacle could have got all these precious materials from in the wilderness turns out to be irrelevant.

Yet there are Christians who will not put aside this practical question so easily. They are convinced that the Israelites there in the wilderness of Sinai had all that gold, silver, bronze and precious stones, acacia wood, scarlet wool and fine linen at their disposal, and even skilled craftsmen who could work with it all. Their argument is that this is what is written and therefore this is what must have happened, since as the word of God the Bible must be historically reliable. I find it very difficult to have a real conversation with these Christians. If I cautiously ask whether they are not approaching ancient Near Eastern literature – for that is what the Bible is – with the modern Western conception of 'objective history writing', they refer to the dogma of the infallible Bible. When I ask about the basis for that dogma, I never get a satisfactory reply. 'That is our starting point,' they say, 'and we don't question it.'

In a debate at the Evangelical High School in Amersfoort I once produced an example which any readers of the Bible can check for themselves. Right at the end of the book of Samuel (II Sam.24) there is the remarkable story in which God himself prompts king David to hold a census. He then wants to punish David for this act. David is to choose one of the three 'classical' disasters, famine, war or pestilence. He chooses the last. While the pestilence is raging he buys the threshing floor of a certain Araunah for fifty shekels of silver (a shekel is about sixteen

20

grams). He builds an altar on the threshing floor, and when he has made a sacrifice there to Yahweh, the pestilence ceases. One of the aims of this story was surely to explain why the temple of Jerusalem was built on this threshing floor of Araunah: David had bought this place, and the sacrifice he had made there had been well-pleasing to God.

After that, I asked people to turn to the book of Chronicles. You can read the same story in I Chronicles 21, but with remarkable differences. There it is not God himself who prompts David to his perverse deed, but Satan. At the end David does not actually buy the threshing floor, but gives the owner 500 shekels of gold. The sacrifice is now no longer consumed by the fire that David has lit, but by a flash of lightning, 'a fire from heaven'. The book of Chronicles was written about 300 by a Jew who had close connections with the temple; he had lost his heart to sacrifice and above all to songs of praise; so he was probably a Levite. He imagined that these had already been dear to the heart of King David, too. So in rewriting the old biblical story he makes the pious king of the twelve tribes of Israel give twelve times the number of shekels to the owner of the threshing floor, not in silver but in gold. He then goes on to make God himself reply to David in a spectacular way, thus confirming at the same time the choice of the site for the temple. Much earlier, the Jewish community had come to feel that one cannot say that God incites anyone to a penal action. That must be the work of another power, Satan, so the writer put this name in place of God in the old story.

This, then, is a clear example of the way in which biblical writers filled out the past, as here, quite boldly introducing modifications from their own time. They use their imaginative power in the service of the faith, which they live out, confess in their writings, and seek to proclaim and communicate to their contemporaries.

The people I was talking with didn't like the term 'imaginative power'. The stories in the Bible are about *facts*, they said. The same amount of money must be meant in the two stories about David and the threshing floor, and an explanation can be found. Yes, it can, if you accept that in the days of the author of Chronicles silver was worth twelve times as much as gold! The author of the old story does not describe the miracle of the flash of lightning, but that could be because he did not know about it, or because he had a reason for leaving out that detail.

I could see no sense in talking further in this way. I was mistrustful and somewhat rebellious. The Evangelical High School had claimed to be a real academic institution. But where the scholarship there relates to the Bible, its only aim seems to me to be to prove the 'historical truth' of the biblical stories. What a waste, I thought; so much intelligence and so much study sacrificed to proving a dogma, a starting point to which people devote no further thought. I was thinking about the many young people I saw there. Over these years of training, as they read the Bible they are being deprived of the possibility of coming into contact with fellow human beings there who have so many different ways of expressing their faith and their life with God.

3   The New Testament Chart: The Origin of the Final Part

On page 25 is the chart which I often draw on a blackboard or sheet of paper when I'm talking about New Testament texts. People are often amazed that the four Gospels were written so long after Jesus. I use this as the occasion for saying something about a number of experiences and insights which were a matter of course to the first Christians, but which are difficult for us to understand and to sympathize with.

First of all, the event denoted at the top, round about the year 30, was regarded by those involved as an earth-shaking experience – in the literal sense of the word. It was a divine work of universal significance, for mankind and for the world. Many Jews in the time of Jesus waited and hoped that God would shortly put an end to this world and its evil powers and that he would make a new world in which he alone would reign. At that decisive turning point in world history he would also raise the dead, at least those who had taken his side in the evil world. Jesus shared this Jewish expectation and had announced that the coming kingdom of God was near. His ignominious end on the cross seemed to prove that he had been deluded. When afterwards he appeared to his disciples and showed himself to be alive, they were overwhelmed by the certainty that he had been right: he had been raised by God from the dead and that meant that God had begun the creation of his new world and would rapidly bring that work to completion. Then the crucified Jesus would appear in 'glory' as the centre and 'Lord' of the created universe.

Those seem to us great words, but many Jews in the time of Jesus thought and spoke in such terms. So there need be no doubt that the followers of Jesus thought and talked about what his appearances meant for them in this 'apocalyptic' imagery. Sadly, we have no direct evidence from them. We do, though, have some from a man who was not one of Jesus' followers, and originally was his enemy, Paul. The crucified Jesus appeared to him as well. In the letters of his which have been preserved, he shows how this experience had shaken his own world. He talks about it in terms of death and life: at that moment the old Paul died and he became a new creation, part of this new world which God had begun by raising Jesus from the dead. It was a kind of mystical experience; from then on his life was governed by a personal relationship with the Jesus who had now been taken up into God. This relationship was of such a kind that at one point Paul exclaims, in his emotional letter to the Galatians: 'In truth, I no longer live, but he lives in me.'

The first generation of Christians thought that the end of this world, this evil aeon, was near and expected that the Lord would appear very soon. Paul was convinced that he himself would personally experience this great turning point. We know that from his letters. From them it also emerges how this theme was part of his preaching and always had a role in his admonitions. He wrote the oldest letter which has been preserved, the first letter to the Christians in Thessalonica, in connection with a problem which had arisen on this point. A recently baptized Christian in this city had died. Hence the anxious question: would Christians like him miss the imminent event? No, replied Paul, don't worry, for those of us who remain alive will not in any way have an advantage over the dead. When the great moment arrives and the Lord appears, first of all the dead who are in Christ will arise and after that those of us who are still alive will meet the Lord together with them.

Because of this expectation, the first Christians really had no reason to put down in writing reminiscences of Jesus' earthly life. People do that above all with an eye to the future, to coming generations. But there was to be no earthly future and no coming generations!

Only in the 70s did the need for putting things down in writing arise. That was not just because the hoped-for 'return of the Lord' seemed so delayed. There was also the fact that those who had been companions of Jesus, those who had seen and

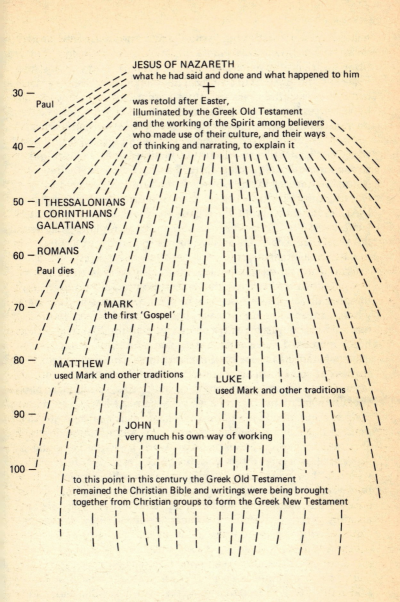

JESUS OF NAZARETH
what he had said and done and what happened to him
✝
30 —
Paul
was retold after Easter,
illuminated by the Greek Old Testament
and the working of the Spirit among believers
who made use of their culture, and their ways
40 —
of thinking and narrating, to explain it

50 — I THESSALONIANS
I CORINTHIANS
GALATIANS

60 — ROMANS
Paul dies

70 —
MARK
the first 'Gospel'

80 —
MATTHEW
used Mark and other traditions
LUKE
used Mark and other traditions

90 —
JOHN
very much his own way of working

100 —
to this point in this century the Greek Old Testament
remained the Christian Bible and writings were being brought
together from Christian groups to form the Greek New Testament

heard him, were beginning to die. Their stories had been handed down so far. Now it was a matter of making a responsible choice from the rich and manifold treasury of stories and sayings of Jesus and putting that in writing. This was all the more necessary because over-enthusiastic narrators of miracle stories about Jesus had sometimes forgotten his real concerns, or rather, God's purpose in his life, ending as it did with his death on a cross.

About the year 70, Mark wrote his Gospel, probably the first work in that totally new genre of biography. For it was quite strange to produce the biography of a man whose life had ended in total failure, an execution which the Romans reserved for the worst criminals. This work by Mark was used by Matthew and Luke when they wrote their Gospels about fifteen or twenty years later. The Gospel of John came into being later still; here the reminiscences of Jesus' life, suffering and death are treated in a quite distinctive way.

I could go on endlessly about the lines on this chart which fan out downwards from the central point. They indicate the handing down of reminiscences of what happened in Jesus and what it meant. Sometimes what was handed down took the form of short phrases, really confessions of faith, like: Men killed him, God raised him up. Alongside that, stories were told which gave substance to these brief exclamations. Those who told the stories did so in Aramaic, the vernacular of the Jews in Palestine, or in Greek, the universal language of the time, which was also spoken by many people in Palestine, where the Jews lived. How people handed down reminiscences of Jesus' earthly life depended not only on the character of those telling the stories but also on the people to whom they were speaking. It made a difference whether these had heard of Jesus before or not, whether they were familiar with the Jewish Bible or not. Furthermore, the framework in whch the stories were told influenced them: stories did not have the same form in a service, in an atmosphere of prayer or contemplation, as they did in encounters where people discussed Jesus and his work.

When it came to handing down short sayings and parables, the memory of the narrators seems to have been very good. Of course they combined their respect for precisely what Jesus had said with a certain freedom to adapt it to new situations, and sometimes to add new sayings to it. For they were convinced that the same Jesus was also speaking to his people now, through disciples empowered to do so by his spirit. Anyone who has studied the ways in which prophetic sayings beginning 'Thus saith the Lord' were handed down and given fixed form in the Old Testament books which bear the names of particular prophets will recognize the same combination of faithfulness and freedom among the disciples of Jesus.

The reminiscences of what Jesus had said and done, and of what had happened to him, were not shaped in quite the same way. Here influences were at work which for the sake of simplicity I shall summarize in three phrases: belief in miracle in the ancient world; the authority of the Jewish Bible; and a sense of symbolism.

As far as the first is concerned, the narrators lived in a culture which believed the world to be permeated by divine forces. There were countless stories in circulation about gods and demigods who had sometimes gone around the human world incognito. In Acts 14 you can read what happened when Paul and Barnabas had healed a lame man in the city of Lystra. People ran up and cried: 'The gods have come down to us in human form!' Priests ran up to these gods and began to offer them sacrifices!

We know from the literature of that time that there were other people who were endowed with divine powers and did amazing miracles. Stories about them were handed down because they attracted people and did not prompt any critical questions. People were not yet thinking in terms of 'laws of nature'. So anything was possible. Ordinary people did not ask whether such and such a miracle was really possible, nor did anyone feel the need to investigate whether the event described really happened. In a conversation about the miracles in the Bible I once thought of an illustration which still seems to me to be quite a good one. Someone in Jerusalem meets an acquaintance and asks, 'Have you heard the latest news?' 'What's that?' 'The mayor of Antioch has turned into a frog.' The other's reaction is not what we would expect, 'That's impossible', or 'Who told you that one?' He simply asks, 'What had he done?' 'Who turned him into the frog?'

I said that the second influential factor on the formation of the stories about Jesus was familiarity with the Bible, the Old Testament, which was soon read in the Greek translation in the majority of Christian communities. It is impossible to over-estimate the importance of this influence on the thought and language of Christians. They regarded this book as a great prophecy, pointing forward in its entirety to the mighty acts of God at the end of time, in which they themselves were involved. Almost all the terms and images they used to denote the person and functions of Jesus came from the Jewish Bible. In Jesus, God had brought about the 'fulfilment' of all that had gone before, of all that was said and done then. He had been announced and described beforehand by Moses, David the Psalmist, and the prophets. Moreover, he surpassed all the men of God in the Old Testament. That book describes how Elijah and Elisha had raised the dead; the same thing could be said of Jesus, with even more justification. According to a story in II Kings 4, Elisha had satisfied the hunger of a hundred men with a few loaves. He had used his miraculous power for the benefit of human beings and had thus provided an 'image' for the one who was to come.

Here we get to what I call a sense of symbolism. By that, among other things I mean the capacity, indeed the habit, of bringing together all kinds of imagery from the Bible and blending it with personal experience. It was said of Jesus that he had 'fulfilled' the miracle of Elisha, that he had satisfied even more people with even less bread with still more left over. This story must have proved very appealing to Christians, because it appears in our Gospels in six different versions. It emerges that narrators also had in mind the miracle of manna in the wilderness. Furthermore, it is clear that when they told how Jesus first said a thanksgiving, or prayer of blessing, then broke the bread, and shared it out among the disciples, they were thinking of the Christian eucharist.

Here's another illustration. In Mark 6 we hear that one evening Jesus forced his disciples to cross the stormy lake in their boat while he went up a mountain to pray. During the night he came to them over the waves and said to them, 'Peace be with you, I am (the one).' As soon as he got into their boat all became calm, both the disciples and the sea.

At first sight this is a strange story. It is strange that Jesus forced the disciples to make this dangerous crossing, and even stranger that he came to them over the water. But when the

28

Christian story-tellers talked about a raging sea and seething waves they and their audience were thinking of the dark powers of disaster and death which raged freely in the human world, and of the God of Israel against whom these dark powers had to yield. A number of psalms depict God in this way as ruler of the raging waters, and in Job 9 it is said that he walks on the tops of the sea, the waves, and that he treads them with his feet. For the church, Jesus has now parted from the disciples and lives with God. He has sent a group of disciples into the turbulent world of the nations, and sometimes they think that he has left them in the lurch and is far away from them. But he represents the saving power of the God of Israel, who as liberator of his people made himself known by presenting himself as 'I am', that is: I am with you and I will not leave you in the lurch. So in the story we have a 'symbolic' expression of what the disciples had experienced. In Jesus the saving power of God is at work, and *at the same time* what they were later able to experience as a Christian community in celebrating his 'memorial', another biblical term which implied more than just a thought of something or someone from the past.

These illustrations must be enough. Of course we shall never succeed in wholly making our own the thought-patterns and expressions of the early Christians. But we can become familiar with them to some degree, and thus understand the meaning of the stories better. Once we have begun to become even slightly familiar with the world in which so many stories about all kinds of miracles were going the rounds, we shall see more clearly what the people of the time saw in the miracle stories which Christians told about Jesus. It must have struck them that this man used his miraculous power solely to deliver people from situations of need, hunger, sickness, danger to life, death. He was never concerned to be spectacular, never asked for money, never revenged himself on people who had threatened or injured him by making them sick or turning them into animals. 'Punitive miracles' of this kind are not told of Jesus. Of course there is one in the Gospels, but that involves a tree! According to Mark 11, one day shortly before his death Jesus uttered a curse on a fig tree near Jerusalem on which he found no figs. When he came past the next day, this fig tree was completely withered. Now in biblical language a tree which bears no fruit is often an image of a man or of the people of Israel when they live fruitlessly, that is, produce no good deeds. There can be no doubt about the symbolic significance of the story of the cursed fig tree, told in the context of Jesus' last vain call for conversion.

Matthew arranges the events of this last week rather differently. For that reason, too, he makes the fig tree wither the moment it is cursed, and this brings out the power of Jesus even more strongly. It is characteristic of Luke that he does not incorporate this one punitive miracle into his story. However, at an earlier point, at the end of chapter 9, he has described how the two disciples James and John wanted a punitive miracle of this kind to be performed on a Samaritan village which had refused to offer Jesus hospitality. A fire was to come down from heaven and destroy these people. Elijah had done something of the sort. That idea was so alien to the spirit of Jesus that the disciples were rebuked firmly for it.

In the instruction which Roman Catholics used to receive, the miracles of Jesus were treated above all as indications of his divine mission: he did things which only God can do, because only God can break the laws of nature which he himself has established. Now that we can read the evangelists' stories in the light of their culture, we can see better what they really wanted to express and communicate by them. You could not talk about someone in whom divine forces were at work, a man of God, indeed a son of God, without describing the miracles that he did. These were part of the picture, the portrait of him. In the portrait of Jesus it must be quite evident that he was always concerned solely for the welfare, the salvation, of men and women.

Those are a few examples of what I usually say in connection with the lines on the chart which run from Jesus to the four Gospels. Often it proves very illuminating. But sometimes I also hear the complaint that it's all very difficult. And the Gospels are meant for ordinary people. Certainly it is always difficult to listen well to someone else, especially when they belong to a distant, foreign culture. You have to devote time and attention if you are going to feel your way into the character, the experiences and the thought-patterns of these others. Inevitably we also face this difficulty in the case of the evangelists. Is learning, academic knowledge necessary? Some can be useful. But I've met very simple people who could sense precisely what a story was really about. Over the course of years they had made that picture, that portrait of the main figure so much their own that they could not misunderstand the meaning of details in it.

4 Jesus the Jew: An Explosion of Humanity

'What was the real aim of this prophet from Nazareth? If it is true that Jesus really wanted to purify and reform Jewish religion in accordance with God's original intentions, how Jewish must Christians really be if they are to understand Jesus well?'

I had to deal with these questions at a meeting of Catholics in Rotterdam. They had been invited as members of the 'Open Church' movement and a good hundred of them were there. I began with a sentence which I have never forgotten since I read it as a student. It was in a book by the great writer H. G. Wells, his *Outline of History*, an account of the whole history of the world from prehistoric times up to and including the First World War. He goes through the whole of history and therefore at a particular point comes to Christ. There he says that he is also trying to write on this subject, too, in such a way that his book can be read as well by Hindus or Moslems or Buddhists as by Americans and Western Europeans. He then gives a short sketch of the figure who emerges from the four Gospels for the unprejudiced reader. In the summary with which he ends, he says that Jesus was too great for his disciples. Jesus spoke in such a way that people felt something terribly strange happening, as though their own world were being swept away. Perhaps the priests and the leaders and the rich people understood him better than his followers. He drove people out of the cosy hideouts into which they had retreated, far from their real human obligations.

In the white-hot glow of his kingdom there was to be no more property, no privilege, no arrogance, no precedence; no other motives and no other aim than that of love. Is it surprising, Wells goes on to ask, that people were bewildered and blinded, and that they were up in arms against him? To accept what he says means beginning a totally new life, embarking on a disturbing adventure. Is it then surprising that even today 'this Galilean is too much for our small hearts?'

Too much for our small hearts. It seemed to me a good idea to begin my introduction with this sentence. No one can fully understand and comprehend Jesus. We can only talk about him with reverence and modesty. Many top figures from our human history were outstanding in particular spheres, as rulers or soldiers or artists, as scientists or philosophers. Jesus did not stand out in any particular sphere of human development. He was great simply as a human being; he was only interested in people and totally concerned with them; that is perhaps the reason why in biblical terms he was called the reflection or the image of God, 'Son' of God. For Jesus was descended from the people of the Bible. He was a Jew, but so much and so totally a Jew that he broke through the limitations of Judaism. I will try to produce some evidence for this statement.

Earlier, Dominicans used to be mocked for their tendency when confronted with any problem whatsoever to go back to its roots. 'You always begin with Adam!' I too have this tendency whenever I talk about Judaism, a relatively late phenomenon. I like to go back much earlier, to the religion of ancient Israel, and really see it against the background of the phenomenon of the other religions of that time. I then tend to ask, 'How did religion really arise?' and then again, 'How did a being who is religious by nature develop from a higher species of animal?' Judaism emerged out of ancient Israel. In comparison with surrounding cultures it is striking how the mystery which human beings sense in and behind all things was experienced in that Israel as 'personal', i.e. in search of relationship, in search of community. In that case, two things were necessarily involved. First, the divine only sought contact with an individual in order to reach his group, with which it wanted to establish a relationship. Secondly, this contact went along with an experience of the divine mystery as saving, willing life, moreover willing life in community. That called for everyone in this group to have a saving and life-giving relationship with the others.

What we can now see from a distance as being essential was not always in the foreground for the people of ancient Israel. National community was experienced in various forms: an agricultural people came to be organized as a monarchy, which after David and Solomon was soon divided into the northern kingdom of Israel and the small kingdom of Judah in the south. The majority of peoples in these areas went through a similar development. It followed as a matter of course that the national deity whom people called Yahweh was given a 'dwelling' next to that of the ruler. This temple had a priestly caste, and society came to be divided into groups and classes: the better off on the one hand and the downtrodden poor on the other. Public opinion always takes that for granted. But in this society there seems to have been a kind of underground tradition which I should want to call pure Yahweh religion. Sometimes this comes to the surface and its voice can be heard in the persons of the prophets. They proclaimed that Israel was to worship Yahweh alone, Yahweh wanted only one thing and he wanted it passionately: a society in which people respected one another, supported one another and cared for one another's well-being.

Amos, from Judah, went to the northern kingdom to protest there, very fiercely, in the name of Yahweh, about the exploitation of the poor. He was then driven out of the land because – the accusation ran – he was preparing an attack on the king. In modern terms, Amos was endangering national security by taking the side of the oppressed. The public generally benefited from the way in which the established order was run. Amos also fulminated against the sacrifices, the liturgy and the songs in honour of Yahweh in the royal temple. He said that Yahweh loathed them and only wanted to see one thing: people letting law and justice flow like a river. The prophet Isaiah expresses the same desire on the part of Israel's God. He tells the famous story about the person who built a vineyard in a prominent place and took a great deal of trouble over the precious vines which he had planted there. He expected outstanding grapes from all his devotion and his care. But what did the vineyard produce at harvest time? Sour grapes, rubbish! By this Isaiah meant that Yahweh had brought Israel into being, had cherished it and cared for it simply because he wanted the fruits of justice and righteousness, a society of people who supported one an-

34

other, gave life to one another, and formed a society which would reflect his nature. They were to be like him, a telling image of him in the world, his 'son'. However, this creative concern only brought him hurt. The produce of his toil and care was injustice and bloodshed.

The prophet then pronounces God's condemnation on people who seize one house after another from the poor, who steal field after field in order to own the land for themselves. These are people who call evil good and what ought to happen bad. They stretch out their hands to him in prayer, still stained with the blood of the innocent. He cannot even bear to look at this scene, and he shuts his ears to it.

A century later Jeremiah announces the destruction of the temple, the dwelling of Yawheh in which people feel themselves to be secure. Yahweh cannot live in this place and feel at home in it, where people are going round ensnaring their neighbours, swearing false oaths, and committing adultery and murder. Jeremiah was arrested because of the way in which he stood up for the real intentions of Yahweh, and he was almost executed; that was prevented only by the last-minute intervention of an influential friend. At that time the northern kingdom of Israel had already been literally wiped off the map for more than a century by the Assyrians. Following their well-tried methods they had scattered the civil population throughout their empire and thus made an end of the nation. Judah underwent the same fate during Jeremiah's lifetime, this time at the hands of the new rulers, the Babylonians. The first deportation took place in 579 BC, and the second ten years later, after the destruction of Jerusalem, the temple, and all the other cities of Judah. Some tens of thousands of people had made the journey into exile of more than a thousand miles on foot, driven on by Babylonian soldiers, through the steppes at the edge of the wilderness. They were allowed to settle in the fields to the south of the capital, Babylon. These people from Judah and Jerusalem were completely shattered. They had been deprived of all support, their homes, their social order, and the monarchy and the temple which had been at the heart of their lives. Above all, Yahweh, the God of their nation, had been done away with. His land had been stripped of its people and his dwelling-place had been destroyed. Evidently he had yielded it to the mighty Marduk and his entourage, the gods of victorious Babylon.

Those who had been deported from Judah were dismayed: there was no more future for them. As they said to one another: 'Our bones are dried up, our hope is fled, it is all up with us...' That was the popular view, public opinion. Even there, however, the undercurrent of pure Yahwism, the true faith, continued to flow. Some dared to rebel against what was commonly felt and said. There, too, the voices of prophets rang out, saying, 'Don't think that Yahweh has lost his dwelling-place. He dwells here; he is here precisely because he is to be found among the crushed and the oppressed. And you are all in that state, because now the king and the merchant and the peasant are all on the same level – they have all been brought down.'

Thanks to these prophets, the exiles increasingly became convinced of something which had never been expressed so clearly before: Yahweh, the God of Israel, is the only God. He is the First and the Last, the Creator and Fulfiller of all things. Beside him there is nothing. Evidently the people had to be stripped of all power and reputation to be able to find their way to such a profound faith. They could no longer express this increasing awareness of faith in a sacrifice, as the temple was far away, and in ruins, and they were in an unclean land. However, they learned to meet together there on the sabbath day and to steep themselves in words from the past and earlier traditions. They emphasized customs which set them apart from patterns of behaviour in the Babylonian empire. They abstained from certain kinds of food and they stressed circumcision, a practice that they had brought with them from Judah which was not current among the Babylonians.

Fifty years after the deportation, Babylon fell into the hands of the conqueror Cyrus, the Persian. He allowed the deported peoples to return home if they wanted to. Thousands of Judaeans went back and rebuilt Jerusalem and the temple. However, most of them remained and gradually spread all over the empire. This was the beginning of Judaism, a people dispersed over the world and kept together by their faith in one God, though Ezra was regarded as its real 'father'. Ezra was a wise scholar who about 400 BC made the Law, the Torah, the foundation of Jewish community life. The day on which he read the

Torah aloud in Jerusalem to the people assembled there has been called 'the birthday of Judaism'. This 'instruction' was not only about God and his world, his humanity and the origin of his own people; it also contained the rules of life which set the Jews apart from all other peoples, Gentiles and idolaters. Here were all kinds of customs aimed at preserving their common belief in the one Creator in the face of other influences in the world in which they also lived. The law is seen as a hedge, a wall round the people, separating the one true God from the heathen.

Justice and righteousness were practised within the Jewish communities. One of the meanings of the word righteousness was what we would call charity, alms, the support of poor Jews and those in need of help. So all over the world they formed close-knit communities, rather like families, whose mutual solidarity was often a source of wonderment. However, sometimes they also provoked opposition by their stand-offish attitude towards non-Jews, on whom they seemed to look down as their inferiors.

Before we come to Jesus it will be useful to know something about what happened to the Jewish community in Palestine in the second century before Christ. The Greek ruler who controlled this area wanted to compel the Jews by force to live in the Greek style and thus to give up those customs which set them apart. He instituted severe penalties for people who had their sons circumcised, observed the sabbath and the food laws, and studied the Torah. Whereas most Jews welcomed this modernization, a small group continued to oppose it from the places where they had gone into hiding. These guerrillas, as we might call them, quickly took up arms against the authorities. Their leader was a certain Judas known as the Maccabee, aided by his brothers Jonathan and Simon, who continued his work when he was killed. These Jews who were faithful to the Law successfully fought against the powerful troops of the occupying forces for the freedom for Jews to follow their own way of life.

This turbulent time had effects right down to the days of Jesus. I shall mention three of them, which influenced his preaching and his fate. First of all was the fact that Jews had shed their blood in the struggle for their customs. So these customs had been made as it were extra sacred by the blood of the martyrs. For these reasons, too, a Jew who cared little for the sabbath and laws about unclean foods, who had criticized sacrifice in the temple, and who did not consider the Torah to be the last word, could be regarded as a traitor to his people.

Another effect of the Maccabean struggle was that Jewish expectations for the future took on new accents. Ancient prophets had dreamed of a divine rule which would extend from Jerusalem and Zion over the whole earth, and which would bring righteousness and peace everywhere. After the exile this became increasingly difficult to imagine. The great events of world history took place elsewhere, far from the unknown city of Jerusalem: decisions were taken in the vast Persian empire, now trodden underfoot by the great Greek Alexander. One of his successors was the Greek prince who sparked off the Maccabean revolt in Palestine with his attack on the Jewish community. He went so far as to desecrate the dwelling of God on earth, the temple in Jerusalem. For believing Jews it was impossible to think of any more direct attack on God. This was the height of wickedness. Their God could only respond by annihilating all the heathen powers completely. And in fact he would do that, soon, and then set up his kingdom, in which all the faithful among his people would share. That included those who had been killed in the fight for the temple and the Torah. They would be raised from the dead. The biblical book of Daniel, completed in 165 BC, bears witness to these expectations. So from then on these ideas were combined: a kingdom which would be established by God himself, of a supernatural kind, one feature of which would be a 'resurrection of the dead'.

Finally there was a third consequence of this struggle for freedom, the rise of a new group, the Pharisees. After the Maccabees had fought on behalf of the Jews for freedom to live in accordance with their own customs, and had thus also achieved a degree of political independence, their successors continued to wage war. Their aim was now to extend Jewish power further, and at one time they ruled over a great deal of Palestine; they had imposed Jewish religion on the population of Galilee by force. From being fighters for religious freedom these men had turned into worldly rulers with pagan mercenaries in their service; at the same time they took over the function of the high priest. At that time, once again, we can see the underground stream of true Yahwism coming to the surface: Yahweh must have nothing to do with militarism and displays of worldly power. This opposition was expressed by people who rejected what public opinion took for granted. They formed groups and parties, like the Essenes, whom we have come to know through the discovery of the place where they lived and their writings, by the Dead Sea. Dispersed over the country, often in brotherhoods, was the party which we know above all from the four Gospels, that of the Pharisees. Their name may be connected with a word which means 'separate'; they were those who had separated themselves from the more worldly majority. They were the most conscientious Jews with whom Jesus came into contact.

When Jesus appeared on the scene, Judah was being governed by the Roman occupying forces, while Galilee and other territories were ruled by a son of Herod who was little more than a puppet of the Romans. There was still a strong expectation, particularly among ordinary people, who suffered severely from the extortion and oppression, that God would 'come' quickly to establish his kingdom. Everyone, every group, filled in the picture in a different way. Jesus also had this expectation. He experienced and proclaimed the fact that God was already active now, realizing his rule in what he himself proclaimed and did. His God was again the God of the old tradition of Yahwism: a God in search of community with men and women, community among men and women. But this emerged more radically than ever: here was a God concerned only for the common salvation of his people. He had a deep abhorrence of everything that erected barriers between them, like riches, power, self-satisfaction, arrogance, discrimination. According to Jesus, you can come near to this God only if you inexorably break down these barriers, even when there are 'religious' reasons for them, even when they are commanded by the old law of God. Indeed this is precisely the time when they should be broken down. For the whole system of communication between God and man through the Torah and customs is a thing of the past. Now God is coming in person with his salvation and speaking directly to men and women.

I need not mention here the great variety of fascinating ways in which Jesus tried to liberate those whom he met from the patterns of behaviour which had become a habit for them, to help them to stop paying attention to what others felt and thought, to make them open to the reality of his God. For by now it should be clear that Jesus had no intention of reforming or purifying Jewish religion, which was the theme of this grouping. He had not come to patch an old garment with new cloth. He sensed that the 'kingdom of God', the final consummation, the ultimate coming of God as king, was close at hand. Indeed it had already begun. He wanted to prepare his people for it, to make them ready for it. He already showed people evidence of the creative power of this kingdom of God, and he invited them to come under its spell.

I said 'his people' deliberately: Jesus did not begin to proclaim that 'coming' of God's kingdom among the Gentile population. He restricted himself to the Jews, and he also expressed the fact symbolically by limiting the number of his immediate helpers to twelve, because twelve was the distinctive number for Israel. The Gentiles are mentioned on very few occasions. For example, they appear in a prophetic threat: they are to come from East and West and enjoy the festal banquet of the kingdom with the patriarchs Abraham, Isaac and Jacob, while those for whom it was really intended, the 'sons' of the kingdom, are to be excluded. The Gentiles also appear in the equally threatening story of the wedding guests who had refused their invitations with all kinds of excuses. So the host told his servants to bring in people from the streets, from the highways and byways, since he was quite determined on one thing, that the room should be full. But in that case those who had been invited first, the Jewish people, would be left out.

It is clear that Jesus went to the root of things, from the heart of God to the depths of man's being, in such a way that all distinctions between people, even those of descent and race, became unimportant.

That brings me back to my starting point. Jesus was Jewish in such a way that he broke through the limitations of Judaism. Let me confess that I have borrowed this view from one of the first Jewish writers to devote a book to Jesus, Joseph Klausner, who had it published in Jerusalem in 1920, in modern Hebrew. Before that time something of this kind had been impossible for a Jew. For Christians revered Jesus as a deity, and the thought of that alone was abhorrent to a Jew: to set a human being on the same level as the one God was a greater blasphemy than even paganism had proved to be capable of. However, from the time of the nineteenth century, with its historical consciousness, Christian scholars had begun to ask what kind of a person Jesus was before he began to be worshipped as the divinized Christ. For thinking Jews there was nothing abhorrent about this historical figure: on the contrary, he attracted increasing attention and respect among them. Many Jews after Klausner began to see him as one of the greatest men in their history. The Jewish thinker Martin Buber called him 'my great brother'. In recent years there has even been talk of a tendency to win back Jesus for Judaism. A German theologian once described this under the fine title *Die Heimholung Jesu ins jüdische Volk*: bringing Jesus home to the Jewish people. There are Christians who welcome this tendency sympathetically. Some people think that familiarity can help them to understand Jesus better. Sometimes the question is raised, 'How Jewish must a Christian be to understand Jesus?'

From what I have said about Jesus' proclamation of 'the kingdom of God', it will have become clear that I feel more at home with Klausner's view. You do not need to be a Jew to be able to understand the message of the kingdom and to accept it. For Jesus appeals to something that is present in every human being.

To end with, I used an illustration to make this even clearer. Jesus had one basic attitude in common with all his believing fellow Jews: we are called to do the will of our Lord and King always and in all things, to obey him in all things and so to bear witness to his rule. However, Jesus differed from the others in his answer to the question, 'What does God want of us?' For all Jews it went without saying that God had laid down his will once and for all in the 613 precepts of the Torah, his 'instruction' which he had revealed through Moses on Sinai. Scholars decided how these regulations were to be adapted in changed and unforeseen circumstances: they devoted their lives to the study of the Torah and the traditional interpretation of it. Jesus said: 'No, it's much simpler than that. At this climax of history God is showing you what he wants of you through fellow human beings who come your way and who need you.' He summed up the whole revelation of God in this one rule: do for others what you would want them to do for you. According to the evangelists, Jesus illustrated this with a reference to the Torah. The Torah says that you must love God with all your heart and mind and soul and strength. Here we must remember that for the Jew of that time, the biblical word 'love' did not primarily denote feelings, as it often does in our language, feelings of affection, being attracted by someone, and so on. Above all it implied dedication in work and deed. 'You must love God with all your heart and all your soul and all your strength' meant: you must be active from first thing in the morning until last thing at night observing God's commandments. Only in that way will you be responding in practice to the love which he has shown to you, his people.

But the Torah also uses the same word for relations with fellow human beings: 'You must love your neighbour as yourself.' Jesus said that this second commandment was as important as the first. So you cannot say that you love God, are really responding actively to his love, if you put yourself before any fellow human being, in any way. No one had ever said this so sharply before. Such teaching was also highly impractical, if you look at it from a lawyer's perspective. The term 'neighbour' was too vague. One lawyer said that he could certainly agree with Jesus that loving one's neighbour actively was an important divine commandment. But you can only fulfil that commandment when you have a precise definition of the term 'neighbour'. Does it mean any fellow-Jew? Or only those who are authentic Jews, who obey the Torah? And where must you go if you want to know whether someone is really faithful to God's commands? Is a superficial impression enough? A lawyer must be able to give precise answers on this question to the pious people who ask him for advice. The law must be 'objective'. So, Jesus, what do you think this term 'neighbour' means?

Jesus' answer was his famous story about the Good Samaritan. He could not have chosen a more shocking illustration. This foreigner, a member of a group which was regarded by any right-minded Jew as profoundly corrupt, appeared to be concerned about the needs of an unknown fellow creature and therefore helped him. 'You must do that too,' says Jesus to this man who devoted his life to studying and teaching the Torah, 'and be neighbour to anyone who needs you.'

Such behaviour cannot be prescribed by a law, because a law determines and thus limits the group which you must love in this way. An interpreter of the law can make that circle larger or smaller. A law is also unsatisfactory because as you go through life you keep having to deal with other people: laws can never lay down how you are to fulfil this duty. Moreover, you can never say that you have really fulfilled it until you are dead. In this way Jesus gave a new interpretation of 'the will of God'. According to him this was so completely concerned with dealings between human beings that 'religious' matters proper seemed to fall outside it. According to the evangelist Matthew, Jesus once painted a picture of the last judgment on all mankind. First they are portrayed as sheep and are separated from the goats. The picture then goes on to treat them as human beings. The heavenly judge asks those who have shown solidarity with the hungry, the vagrants, the sick and the captives to join him. He does not say anything at all about their 'religious' life. The only norm which he applies is whether or not they have helped people in need.

If we are to be able to understand Jesus, we evidently need only to be human beings. We are challenged by him to show solidarity with our fellow human beings and in this way to make sense of our lives. Jesus himself remained faithful to his preaching, and in actual practice lived out what he saw as the authentic, original intentions of God. He kept faith at the cost of his life. We believe that God also kept faith with him and that this great Galilean from the distant past has gone before us, continuing to challenge us to be more human to one another.

After this introduction there was a break. The participants went off in small groups to discuss their comments and questions and to agree on how to express them. From the papers that came back it seemed that there were three main themes that people wanted to talk about further: how Jesus dealt with the Old Testament; the role of that book in our society; and whether we do not have to learn from the Jews here, because the Old Testament is their book.

On one of the papers the question was put like this. Can you go more closely into the way in which Jesus interpreted the Old Testament? No, was my answer, because he never did this! He did not see it as his task to interpret old texts; indeed I myself feel that he scarcely knew the Old Testament.

Before I go into this, there is one piece of information we need to have. We know of Jesus only what his disciples remembered. This would be what they found distinctive enough to remember, things that made an impression on them. Now that will be only a fraction of all that he had said and done. Furthermore, the evangelists made a selection from the reminiscences which were still current in this first generation. Anyone who takes the trouble to read Luke alongside Mark, the Gospel which Luke used when he wrote his own, can confirm that: he sometimes leaves out reminiscences of Jesus' words and deeds recorded in Mark, evidently because they did not fit into the picture which he had formed and wanted to pass on to his readers.

There is something else to add. Everyone knows that a memory is a living thing, bound up with the person who retains it. Memories are not recorded mechanically, like photographs or tapes. When people 'recall' a memory, as they tell of it they also say something about what they are and what they experience now. It is the same with the reminiscences of Jesus. Anyone who reads the first three Gospels one after another can establish that sayings of Jesus were often handed down in many different forms. A good example is the prayer which Jesus taught: read the 'Our Father' in Matthew 6 alongside the version in Luke 11.

Now over the last few decades biblical scholars have developed methods of getting behind the reminiscences related in the Gospels and coming as close as possible to the original impressions, in other words to what bystanders would really have heard and seen. For example they have worked out the earliest form of the parables, the most characteristic form of Jesus' teaching. What struck these scholars was that nothing in the parables comes from the Old Testament. Jesus borrows the figures in the parables, like all the imagery he uses in his short sayings, from his immediate surroundings, from the world which is familiar to himself and his audience. Think of the landowner and his wily steward, the farmers, the fishermen, the merchants and the tax collecters, the pious Pharisees, poor widows, whimpering children; the friend who turns up unexpectedly, the men in search of work hanging around in the market place. And there are also the oil lamp in the room, the sparrow on the roof, the flowers by the wayside, the ox who slips when drinking and falls into the water. Not a trace of biblical texts! Of course Jesus knew the ten commandments, as any child did, and great names like those of the patriarchs and Moses and David, along with a few unforgettable stories, like those of the flood and of Jonah in Nineveh. But the earliest reminiscences do not suggest that he was preoccupied with the Old Testament.

Someone in the room interrupted me: 'But Jesus read some of the prophet Isaiah in the synagogue of Nazareth and explained the text! That's in Luke 4!'

I patiently took time to show why Jesus' use of the Bible in this story is a product of imaginative Christian meditation. First I read the earlier story of Jesus' visit to Nazareth from Mark 6, a version which Luke had in front of him. Jesus began by teaching in the synagogue there. We are not told what he taught. However, the people asked themselves where he got this wisdom from. After all he was the carpenter, and everyone knew his parents and brothers and sisters. Then Jesus remarked that a prophet is not recognized among his own people. Mark ends by saying that he was unable to heal many sick people there in Nazareth because of their lack of faith.

Evidently Luke found that story rather too thin. He wanted to make more of it, first by filling in what Jesus had taught in the synagogue. So he took a text from Isaiah 61 which was much beloved in the Christian circles in which he moved, and rightly so! In it the prophet declares that the Spirit of God is upon him, and that he has been 'anointed' by God to bring the message of salvation and liberation. This is what Jesus read:

The Spirit of the Lord has come upon me
because he has anointed me.
He has sent me to bring the Good News to the poor,
to proclaim their release to prisoners,
to make the blind see,
to let the oppressed go free,
and to proclaim the Lord's year of grace.

The precise words of this text cannot be found in translations of Isaiah from the original Hebrew. Luke quotes it from the rather different Greek translation, and in order to make it more complete he reads in a phrase from Isaiah 58 ('to let the oppressed

45

go free'). You can also see from this that Jesus cannot have read this text as it stands from a Hebrew scroll.

Furthermore, Luke also expanded the end of Mark's story with the help of the Old Testament. He makes Jesus refer to two stories about prophets from the biblical book of Kings. During a long drought, many widows in Israel were at death's door because of famine. With his miraculous power Elijah came to the rescue of one of them from outside Israel, a Gentile woman in Sareptah, near Sidon. Elisha did something of the same sort; there were a great many lepers in Israel, but the prophet healed Naaman the leper, a Syrian from Damascus. When the people of Nazareth heard this, they were angry and tried to lynch Jesus, but he escaped unscathed.

These two stories were very significant for Christians because of their experiences at the time when Luke was writing: at that time the message of God's love, 'the gospel', was being proclaimed to non-Jews beyond the borders of Israel and outside the Jewish communities dispersed around the world. These non-Jews accepted this message as an unexpected benefit. The majority of Jews were angry about this. In the stories about Elijah and Elisha, who showed God's benevolent and miraculous power at work among the Gentiles, Christians saw a foretaste of their own experiences, and they evidently felt no hesitation at all about expressing this through Jesus.

With the help of these extra biblical details, Luke not only made the short account in Mark 6 more profound and more dramatic; at the same time he made it more suitable to put at the beginning of Jesus' public ministry. The quotation of the text from Isaiah made Jesus' preaching in the synagogue into a kind of inaugural address. And the way in which the people of Nazareth rejected him was a prelude, as it were, to the later course of Christian preaching which Luke wanted to go on to describe in the second part of his work, the Acts of the Apostles.

Jesus' knowledge of the Bible was introduced into the reminiscences of his career as an 'afterthought'. That is quite understandable. Many other Jews soon joined the followers who recognized him after Easter as Messiah. Among them there were certainly also scribes who knew the Jewish Bible back to front, either in the Hebrew text or in the ancient Greek translation of it. In the light of their new faith, or rather, of the new interpretation of their old faith, they saw 'prophetic' references to Jesus, to his preaching and his way of life, his cruel death and his resurrection, in many texts. And the number of these texts steadily increased. In the Jewish culture of that time it was not so strange as it might seem to us now that people read the Bible as a prophecy of their own experiences. The Essenes did that too. Far less did people have doubts about attributing a detailed knowledge of these biblical texts to Jesus, who was so completely filled with God and his holy Spirit. Luke in particular does this at the end of his Gospel, in the story of the men on the road to Emmaus: Jesus himself explained to these two men what the scriptures said about him, and later he instructed his group of close followers in all that was written about him in 'the law of Moses, the prophets and the Psalms'.

However, from the earliest reminiscences there emerges a Jesus who knows no more about the Bible than the next man. I recently read a short article in a scholarly journal on the Bible about Jesus' identification of the two commandments which I mentioned in my introduction: love God and love your neighbour. The writer began by recalling a feature which was prominent in the Jewish exposition of the Torah. Because this text was dictated by God himself to Moses, no word, no letter, could be there by chance. Everything had to have a profound meaning. For example, if God uses a particular term or phrase in the story of the journey through the wilderness, and it occurs in precisely the same way in the story of Abraham, God must have had something in mind. It is up to the scholar to discover the link between these texts. As early as Jesus' time there was endless study of the significance of such links between texts, and they were discussed constantly.

Now as the writer of this article observed, the Hebrew verb-form 'you must love...' occurs only twice in the Torah: once with God as object and the other time with the neighbour as object (Deut.6.5; Lev.19.10). Jesus will have said to the scribe: 'You have spent all your life discovering all kinds of subtle associations in the sacred texts relating to incidental matters, while here God himself is identifying these two commandments in the simplest way of all: you must love God *and* you must love your neighbour. It's the same love in each case. God makes that quite clear, and you have overlooked it.'

At first sight this attracted me. It seemed to me to be authentically in the style of Jesus, and to be saying something like this: 'You get so lost in unimportant matters that you miss the wood for the trees.' However, on further reflection it appears to me highly improbable that Jesus knew the Hebrew Bible well enough to be able to make such an observation. I would rather attribute this to a Jewish scribe who had become a Christian. Otherwise you would have to suppose that Jesus had also learned the ancient Hebrew of the Bible as well as his mother tongue, Aramaic; in other words, in our terms, that he had studied 'theology'. In that case, could he have identified himself so closely with ordinary people, and could he have expressed himself in such a 'popular' way? Of course, people say that Jews who spent their time studying the Torah also took on work to support themselves, and that the 'Rabbi Jesus' was a professional carpenter to earn his living. But in that case the people of Nazareth would not have been so amazed at the learning of their carpenter.

Jesus did not appeal to biblical texts, but to common sense and to what people could see for themselves. 'God makes his sun shine on good and bad alike. He gives his rain to the just and the unjust.' That's obvious! If you want to be a child of this Father, then do the same thing: be generous without first asking whether the person to whom you are giving deserves it. Give freely, as you see that God does.

The Torah commanded that wicked Israelites, those who transgressed God's law, were to be thrown out of the community. No one was to have anything to do with them. But that is precisely what Jesus did. Not only did he talk to 'tax collectors and sinners', but he ate and drank with them. In this culture, having a meal together was a much stronger expression of deep solidarity than it is with us. So Jesus went against one of the precepts of the Torah. He knew better: God himself has not written off these people. He loves them unconditionally. And they could only feel that through a fellow human being who accepted them whole-heartedly and therefore made them feel that they were worth while, even to God, and were true members of 'his' people.

By joining in these meals Jesus ran the risk of becoming impure, through contact with people who had become impure, and above all through eating impure foods. The Torah contained a number of rules about this, which were classified and made more precise by the interpreters of the law: they determined what food made people 'impure', i.e., unfit to worship God, and what these people had to do to become pure again. This was an extremely important matter for a Jew who was faithful to the Law. 'That can't be right,' says Jesus. 'What you eat goes into your mouth and then comes out again as excrement. It's nothing to do with the heart! And that's the only place where you come up against God; that's where your conscience lies and that's where God appeals to you.'

Jesus was equally simple and clear on the question of observing the sabbath, the day on which Jews were not allowed to do any work. There were countless rules which determined what counted as work. He saw these rules for what they were. The sabbath is God's day, so even more than on the other six days you must do all you can on this sabbath to help your fellow human beings.

From his own experience of God as Father Jesus developed a new pattern of personal relationships, and remained faithful to it. The main characteristic of his life-style was giving and sharing, being prepared to forgive harm done and not striking back, being open towards others, unprejudiced, ready always to see other people with new eyes. In that new society there were to be no more rulers and no more subjects. On the contrary, all were to be brothers and sisters, children of the Father. Anyone who wanted more had to do what Jesus himself had already done: he served his disciples at table. He saw his whole life as service to men. His death, too, was a service towards the coming kingdom of God. He was full of confidence that this form of society would come, as God's work which was at the same time wholly performed by men. Anyone in search of that kingdom of God will find it, he says, just like the merchant in search of a precious pearl. When he found it, he sold all that he had in order to buy the pearl. The same experience may also just happen to people, as in the case of the man who came upon a treasure in the field where he had to work. 'For joy at this he sold all that he had and bought this field.' I can never hear this story without sensing some of Jesus' own delight in it, his joy at knowing that he was so loved by God and that with this love he could kindle the hearts of other people, as it were with a kind of fire. This is the joy of someone who lives in complete trust and wants to express it: trust in God and at the same time trust in the common sense of human beings and the value of their deepest longings.

I ended by saying that Jesus was not concerned about the Bible and that he did not work with biblical texts. He knew God in his heart and was confident that any human being could be open to him. When I said that, I immediately thought of a passage from Jeremiah 31: a time will come when people will no longer have to deal with the will of God from a written text that has to be learnt, because by then everyone will know from within what God requires. If Jesus had known the Bible he would surely have quoted this text: that was precisely what he was saying!

This observation brought us to the second theme. How far as a Christian do you have to be at home in the Old Testament? After everything I had just said, my answer could be very short: if you want to understand the New Testament authors well, you need to have some acquaintance with the Old Testament. That was their Bible, and in it they found the words and images used by God himself to show that he was involved in this new and latest phase of his history with mankind. But I provoked a deal of perplexity by my emphasis on the 'if': *if* you want to understand the New Testament well... You may prefer that, to occupy yourself with the Bible in that way, and that is a good choice. But if you don't have the time or the opportunity for it, or if it doesn't interest you very much, that doesn't mean that you're any the less a believing Christian. For to believe as Jesus understood it is a way of life, a way of responding to God and your fellow human beings, and these two things cannot be separated. So belief is an everyday affair. I had just read something in a new book by Johanna Klink, a well-known specialist in the field of biblical education for children, on which she has written a good deal, a comment that Jesus had never written anything down, but knew God as a son knows his father. 'If putting things down in writing was of such decisive importance, then he should have been the great writer *par excellence*. Moreover, we do not have a single saying of Jesus in which he commands his apostles to write down what he said or what he did.' I felt that this book by Dr Klink showed some resistance to excessive praise of the Bible and thus also to a feeling that we have to keep going back to it. I often find myself feeling the same resistance. I recall a rather scornful remark made by an English theologian: Christians officially confess three divine persons, but when you see and hear them at work, what emerges is, 'I believe in the Father, the Son and holy scripture!'

I myself once expressed this resistance in a short article which was to appear at the end of a large illustrated edition of the Bible in seven parts. I had to answer the question which I had been given as the title: 'What do I do with the Bible?' In that very short space I had written something about the origin of the Bible, and had then given a few illustrations of how not to use it. I pointed out how in the course of centuries violence has been done to all kinds of people and has been justified by references to the Bible. I mentioned the Negroes, the Jews, homosexuals and, in our time, the Palestinians.

Not only does every heretic have his text, but even orthodox believers can always find a text in the Bible to justify their actions. Shortly beforehand I had read in the paper what had happened in a respectable Reformed congregation in Rotterdam. During the service, the minister had commented on the presence of a youth with long hair. After the service, he explained why he had commented. 'Scripture teaches clearly that people may not have long hair. We can only go by scripture, and this must be our guideline.' That sounds partly pious and partly dishonest and hypocritical! It would have been more honest to say: 'Respectable citizens like us do not want any long-haired types in our congregation; we find that offensive.' The biblical text they were referring to occurs in a passage from a letter of Paul's which is rather difficult to follow, in I Corinthians 11. There he says, 'Does nature itself not teach you that it is a scandal for a man to wear his hair long?' That was evidently the masculine fashion in the Graeco-Roman world of Paul's time and philosophers discussed it in the kind of way illustrated by Paul in his complicated argument. But what nonsense it is to take such an observation as a 'guideline' in any situation! I suddenly thought that the solemn and pious gentlemen who in the years before 1637 worked on the Dutch translation of the Bible, which was called the *Statenbijbel*, all had long hair. That was the fashion in that century. I asked myself what these believers, who were so faithful to the Bible, did with Paul's comment. I looked up their rendering of it, and indeed they had no difficulty in making the text innocuous. They observed that nature had certainly distinguished the feminine gender from the masculine, among other things by making the hair on women's heads grow longer and thicker than that on men's heads.

That sort of thing makes me feel: 'If only the Bible would cease to exist!' I sometimes think that, in rebellious moments. It is a book which makes it so easy for us to persevere in our prejudices, to maintain our familiar standards, our selfishness, our desire for money and lust for power. It is seldom the case that the Bible has 'power', that it 'makes itself felt', and so on, as they say in Protestant circles.

And yet the Bible is a 'powerful' book. There is no other book in which so many people have a say, in which they have put into words their experience of the mystery that we call God. This mystery is so utterly exalted and yet at the same time involves us, coming close and challenging us to form a true community. All these people in the Bible have some connection with the central figure, Jesus, who was described in the four Gospels. These form a very special kind of literature, unparalleled anywhere in the world. For no one else has been granted the power to affect the lives of so many people after his death.

I had been asked to answer the question, 'What do I do with the Bible?' This is what I suggested as a practical answer: You can teach people to have a feeling for what those who told these ancient stories really meant; you can put yourself in the place of particular figures; you can go with Abraham on the way to the unknown destination which you have been promised, and with an exhausted Elijah to the mount of God, in order to gain new strength.

You can learn to believe after the fashion of Hosea and Isaiah and Jeremiah. In the dark hours of your life, when you simply cannot go on, and you look desperately for meaning, you will find fellow sufferers in passages of the Psalms and the book of Job. You can learn to listen to the Gospels in 'stereo', in order to distinguish the voice of Jesus himself from those whom he attracted to him, while at the same time hearing them together, and in this way you will be taken up into the first, vigorous life of the movement to which you, too, want to belong.

But at the same time you are constantly directed towards the people around you. Suppose that after years of dealing with the Bible you can say that you have learned to understand the distinctive language of all these writers, and that you know the book well. You will still come up against what a disciple of Jesus says to you: 'Though I speak with the tongues of men and of angels and have not love, I am nothing.' In that case the book itself (I Cor.13) directs you away from the book towards your fellow men. For only in dealing with them can it emerge that you are merciful, that you are not envious, and do not take account of evil.

Only there, in our dealings with others, does the Lord of the Bible reveal what he wants of us here and now. And even though we may have a large illustrated Bible of this kind in a bookcase, in seven imposing volumes, we may suddenly think of a saying of Jesus about giving away everything that we possess.

The end of my contribution went like this: 'So the institution in which the Bible is to be read requires that we should be prepared for any kind of "conversion" in our relationship with the people around us. Approached in this way, the Bible can play its part in the great adventure with God, and no one will ever be able to say that he turned his back on it.'

In the conversation which followed, an elderly women made everyone laugh by observing that she thought that I was a real Catholic. 'That's what we used to have in our Catechism,' she said: 'Reading the Bible isn't necessary, but it's useful!'

It was too late to go in detail into the third series of questions about the Jews, namely whether we can learn something from them about reading the Old Testament, which after all was their book first. Nor can I go into it in detail here. So I contented myself with a few points that I feel you have to think about when this question comes up. First of all, you can hardly talk about 'the Jews' as if these were always roughly the same and expressed their belief in the same way. That is even less the case with 'Christians'. Among Christians, too, you find the most divergent and sometimes even contradictory ideas. When I hear about conversations, religious conversations between Jews and

Christians, I always ask myself, 'Which Jews are talking to which Christians?'

Secondly, when it comes to reading the Bible, remember that no individual is a blank page, or, to put it in a different way, can read without a particular perspective. A Jew cannot rid himself of two thousand years of reading in the Jewish tradition, and it is the same with Christians. Of course at present it is possible to use all the means of historical scholarship to discover what a biblical writer intended to say in a particular passage and what he sounded like to his contemporaries. But this approach cannot achieve a degree of certainty which convinces everyone, precisely because it is historical, and historical certainty is a different kind of certainty from academic proof. But above all, it is the Jews and Christians with traditional faith, the 'orthodox', who do not want to take this course, this academic approach to the study of biblical texts.

Perhaps an authentic conversation between a Jew and a Christian about their faith is possible only when both of them have listened honestly and patiently to what lies at the very depth of each of their traditions. And if that happened it would be best if their conversation could end in silence, in their both being seized by the mystery of God.

5   A Letter to India

'Your Jesus has been dead for two thousand years. I can see and hear mine, he speaks to me and looks at me.' That is what Karin said to me when she came to say goodbye. She had decided to go and live permanently in India, with her master, the Bhagwan. I knew her and her husband before they got married. He was training to be a commercial pilot. When he had his qualifications he spent the days he was not flying studying psychology. His wife was active in therapeutic groups. They were genuine, lively people and I liked meeting them.

One day Karin got hold of a book by Bhagwan. It fascinated her so much that she went off to find him and immediately came under his spell. After a while her husband went to look for her, but he found the set-up around the Bhagwan very strange.'Joop thinks too much,' said Karin, 'and you've got to stop doing that if you want to be open to what the Bhagwan has to offer.' I listened to her stories for some hours and made virtually no comment on them. Perhaps she saw in my eyes the question whether she had got to the stage of being prepared to leave behind her husband and children. At all events, she said: 'Your Jesus said that too, that you must leave everything, even your family, if you were called by him.' As she was leaving, she took a book out of her bag. 'I thought about you a great deal there, Grol, and I bought this book about Jesus by Bhagwan for you.' I felt that was most thoughtful of her. The coloured cover showed Bhagwan, modestly walking along a woodland path, with a young woman behind him. The title was: *Come Follow Me. Talks on Jesus*.

Karin took the name Prartho, which means 'She who prays'. The following summer she paid a visit to Holland. The meeting we arranged fell through. Some months later I got a postcard from her. The photograph showed Bhagwan on a kind of platform, his hands folded on his breast, and around him hundreds of people looking at him rapturously, also with their hands folded in front of them in the same way. On the back was printed in English: 'This commune is not an ordinary commune. This is an experiment to provoke God.' Underneath Karin had written: 'Dear Grol, This time you missed me in Holland. So now it's your turn to come here. You can't not come. You can't miss something so fantastic in your life. Grol, I have such a fantastic life here, people are so full of energy and loving. Bye, lots of love, Prartho.'

After looking at this card and reading it, I began a letter to her straightaway.

Dear Karin,

Even if I had the time and the money, I wouldn't come to Poona. You believe that you've found paradise with Bhagwan, particularly now you know that Joop and the children are getting on all right without you. Even apart from your account, I've now heard and read so much about life there in the commune that I don't feel any need to come and experience that paradise. You know that I was really open when you first told me about Bhagwan and I even read some of the books and papers that you gave me. I found him an exceptionally gifted man, and still do. The practical wisdom that he has read and thought up and made his own verges on the incredible. And so does the way in which he can express all this in his daily talks. It's a brilliant mixture of profundity and humour. Every day a new one-man show. I can imagine how people can be attracted by this man, even 'captivated' by him in the literal sense of the word. He seems to find this captivity to his person necessary for the happiness of his disciples. He has also gathered exceptional colleagues around him so that they can use their skill in all kinds of group work to liberate people from tensions and inhibitions and taboos. Here too he has made a careful selection from ancient Eastern practices and modern Western techniques. He certainly does this to liberate people, but at the same time to impose a new bondage on them, a bondage to him, Bhagwan, so that they always wear *his* portrait round their necks and dress in *his* favourite colour.

56

That's one of the things that I can't take. Bhagwan thinks he's important, allows himself to be worshipped, even if he may perhaps say in so many words that this isn't the case. In my view, that's not the mark of a truly religious person. When you were with me, you compared Bhagwan to Jesus. One of the oldest stories in the Gospels tells how someone fell on their knees before him and asked, 'Good master, what must I do to obtain eternal life?' Jesus reacted angrily to that reverential tone. 'Don't call me good! Only God is good.' I don't see Bhagwan reacting in that way.

I accept, Karin, that he wouldn't be able to react in these terms anyway, because he belongs to quite a different religious world from Jesus. The Jews experienced the divine as personal, as Someone at work in everything, yet different from it all. So their religion was determined by this personal God, and this tradition was taken over by Christians and Moslems. In the religions of India the divine was not seen in so personal a way; it was so to speak dispersed over the cosmos, in things and in people. It was present in some people in a very concentrated way, especially in those who had arrived at 'enlightenment'. Bhagwan must also have had this experience. It is said that he did, and I see no reason for doubting it. So he felt divinity in himself and he also emanated it. Westerners who surrender themselves to him can also feel this divine 'energy' in themselves, like the emanation you described, and they experience the way in which it makes them happy and brings them liberation. So Bhagwan can allow himself to be revered, since for him this means accepting veneration of the divinity that is in him. If I remember rightly, Bhagwan himself calls this emanation around him a 'Buddha field', and does not want to leave India because something of the kind is possible only in that country.

But as well as this difference in culture I see many other differences between Bhagwan and Jesus. First of all, if you want to have access to Bhagwan you have to be sniffed at all over, because he can't bear any smells and odours. He wants clean people around him. In the stories about Jesus you can sometimes see him knocked flat by an oppressive mass of people. He touches the sick and the lepers. Evidently no person is too filthy for him.

Furthermore, the stories about Jesus give the impression that people were constantly demanding his time and that it was only at night that he could find any solitude to pray. He went round with his little group of disciples from one place to another and shared his life with them. He had no private life. That's very different from Bhagwan. He has a villa of his own some distance from the commune and it's said that no outsiders are allowed into it. But you will know that better than I do.

Of course I sometimes see a parallel when I read how Bhagwan spices his teaching with all kinds of surprising stories and anecdotes which often make people laugh. Jesus also did that, and there was doubtless a good deal of laughter when he was around, certainly at the droll comparisons which he sometimes made. If you are constantly pointing out what other people are doing wrong, then you're like someone busy taking a splinter out of another person's eye who fails to see that he has a beam in his own eye! I'm also thinking of the remark about the fly and the camel. Here you need to know that the life of the pious Jew was strongly influenced by a concern to avoid all kinds of impurities which according to the Law would exclude him from worship; Jews could become unclean by eating the flesh of certain animals. These included pigs and many other animals, the largest of which was the camel. Touching a dead body was also forbidden. There could be a dead fly in a cup of milk, so pious people sieved their milk to make quite sure. In the meantime they fiercely condemned all the other Jews who did not observe the laws of purity so scrupulously: 'You aren't fit for God.' 'Well, well,' said Jesus once, 'you sieve out the fly and swallow the camel.' Something of this kind would certainly have provoked loud laughter. Years ago the English author Dennis Potter wrote a television play about Jesus in which Jesus often laughed and joined in the laughter of others. He was a real 'Son of man', as the title of the play went. This was a good corrective to the earnest solemnity in which so many people have cherished their picture of Jesus. They had forgotten that he was fond of sitting at table with people who in the eyes of authentic pious Jews were wicked, transgressors of God's law, sinners. They ate and drank together, and Jesus celebrated with these people the gift of life, sharing with them what we need to sustain it. This was how he shared with them the goodness of the God who gives and forgives, in an atmosphere of joy.

So I do see some similarity between our masters on this point, a free inner joy which makes people happy. But do you remember, Karin, what you said to me about Jesus having been dead for two thousand years while you can see and hear and touch your master? You may think it crazy, Karin, but this Jesus from so long ago speaks to me much more strongly than Bhagwan will ever be able to, even if I could sit there in the tent in front of him every evening. I don't in fact know what Jesus looked like, whether he was tall or short, fat or thin, whether he had a beard or not, whether his hair was dark or fair, whether he was an attractive man or an ugly one. All I know is that he did not stand out from the group of Galileans who were with him. Judas had to arrange with the police to identify Jesus to them in the twilight of the garden by kissing him. You can see Bhagwan every evening, a particularly attractive man with those evocative eyes and all those different expressions on his face. I've seen hundreds of different pictures of him in the paper published by the movement and in the books which you gave me, sometimes very attractive ones.

But although I do not know what Jesus looked like, what stands quite clearly before me is his personality, everything that motivated him. I can see what he wanted, how on the basis of his relationship with God he spoke to people and dealt with them, reacted to them. He remains very much alive to me; he continues to attract me through the gospel stories which I keep reading and hearing, and also through people in whom I can recognize something of him. There are Christians from the past who have written about their life of faith and Christians whose biographies have been written. I could give you a whole list of books which have been my favourite reading over the course of my life. There is a kind of chain of Christians through whom I continue to have contact with the beginnings of Christianity.

But above all there are people around me who keep adding to my picture of Jesus by the way in which they live. They put into practice what he wanted and what he lived for. I see them doing that by their respect for others, by patience and forgiveness and infectious trust, by their dedication, sometimes in the context of their daily work, sometimes in public, in their activity on behalf of the poor and weak in their immediate neighbourhood or in the Third World, in action for peace – to mention just a few things. Where I see dedication to the cause of humanity I see Jesus, even though his name is not mentioned. It does not even need to be. He is said once to have painted a picture of the last judgment in which all kinds of people were invited to share in the joy of being with God, people who had never heard of Jesus. There is no need, he said, for you have helped fellow human beings in need and as a result you have become part of the family of God.

For many Christians, and I include myself among them, the picture of Jesus remains alive and attractive above all through the celebration of the last supper, the eucharist. As we pray, we remind God of what Jesus did on the evening before his passion, before the death that awaited him because he had championed so radically the true happiness of human beings. What he did that evening was to pass bread and wine round the table as a sign of his total dedication to his God who wanted to bring men together in a new alliance. As together we eat that bread and drink from that cup in which he gives his whole self, we experience his presence in a very direct way. Perhaps in the same way as you already recognize a friend by approaching footsteps before the knock at the door. But that comparison is too weak.

Along with Bhagwan you talked about an energy-world, tangible in the commune where you now live. We might perhaps also use that term for what emanated from Jesus, but without the limitations of space and time.

That's where my letter stopped. I put it aside for a while. When I read it again I found that it really said far too little, and at the same time far too much. It might perhaps offend Karin. Then I heard that Bhagwan had left India and had set up a great project somewhere in the United States. This indicated that he had quite clearly, as the report said, 'gone on a commercial tour'. This report confirmed what I had not put in my letter: that Bhagwan struck me as being so Western, so extravert, a showman with a talent for organization. I saw so little in him of what attracts me in the culture of India and sometimes makes me rather jealous, because we miss it so painfully, so disastrously in our Western world. By that I mean a sense of the importance of inwardness, the concern that a person must have to seek ways to his or her deepest self, to that innermost part where they come into contact

60

with their origin, the source of their existence. I did not put that in my letter. But after that report I no longer had any reason to send it.

6   About the Divinity of Christ

For some years now I have been taking part in a discussion group with a number of Catholic couples, some of them with children who are almost grown up. Recently we were going to spend an evening talking about the Christian confession of faith, the 'creed'. Most of those taking part seemed to have a great deal of difficulty with this text. The first sentence, 'I believe in God, the Father Almighty, Maker of heaven and earth', was all right. But 'Jesus Christ his only Son our Lord,' was already much more difficult, certainly with the 'Holy Spirit' as the third part. One of the people present, an engineer, thought it sheer speculation, this three persons in one God.

Above all there was resistance to 'I believe in the holy catholic church'. How can you believe in a Roman institution which claims to be the only true church? 'Do we really have to believe, Lucas, that there is no salvation outside the church? And this institution still goes on calling itself holy!' There was great amazement when I said that this creed came from the second century of the Christian era. Did it already have the phrase 'catholic church' in it then? 'Certainly,' I said, 'this expression was already used by Bishop Ignatius of Antioch, who was martyred round about 117.' There was even more amazement when I recalled that the three 'divine persons' are already mentioned together in the Gospel of Matthew, at the end, when Jesus gives his last command. I read it out: 'Go and make disciples of all nations and baptize them in the name of the Father and of the Son and of the Holy Spirit, and teach them to observe all the commandments that I give you.' Where this command had a successful outcome, where people resolved to become disciples of Jesus and to have their resolve confirmed through baptism, the church came into being. That word comes from the Greek *kyriak(on)*, which means something that belongs to the *kyrios*, the Lord, a group of people who are oriented on him. The intention is that this group oriented on Jesus shall put down roots and extend among all peoples, so that the 'church' finally becomes universal, all-embracing, the Greek for which is 'catholic'. This was the aim from the beginning, and that is why the term appeared in the old confession of faith,

But now back to Jesus. Evidently Matthew already regarded him as a divine person. 'How can that be?', they asked. 'You keep saying that the New Testament is a Jewish book. And for a Jew it is impossible to identify a man with God in this way. The Greeks and Romans were used to the idea that great men were the offspring of deities, sometimes the sons of divine couples, and also that at the end of their lives people were taken up into the divine world. But for the Jews with their belief in one God who is so infinitely far above all that he has created, utterly alone in his holiness, his otherness, something of the kind was inconceivable.'

In reply, I made the point that the divinization of Jesus, to call it that, had come about within the framework of biblical thought. Here I could refer back to earlier discussions I had had with this group. We had been talking about a Jewish way of thinking which lies behind some biblical stories. In our language we have terms for indicating that something, for example a particular practice, is very important for our social life: in that case we say that it is of *fundamental* importance or of *basic* significance. When we use these words we hardly ever still think of the particular concepts from which they are derived: the foundation of a building or the basis on which something rests. The biblical writers were unable to do this sort of thing, to use terms in which the original concept or thing had ceased to be suggested by the word. In other words, abstract thinking was alien to them. They had a different way of expressing the fundamental significance of a particular practice. To convey that, they said that it already existed at the beginning, in ancient times, when so to speak the foundation of society was laid. I had mentioned circumcision as an example. Those who had lived in the kingdom of Judah had been deported to Babylon in 587, and there they stood out because they were circumcised, a custom that was unknown to the Babylonians. So, for the Jews, being circumcised became a sign by which they were visibly linked with one another and with their God; it became a kind of token of that covenant. They indicated its great importance by telling how God had already commanded Abraham to be circumcised as a sign of the divine covenant with him and his descendants. The second example I gave was the sabbath, which at the time of the exile began to take on the central significance that it was always to have in Jewish life. Therefore it was said that that day was established at the very beginning of the world: God himself, they related, performed his work of creation in six days and rested on the seventh day, the sabbath.

After I had recalled these illustrations I asked the group to listen to a passage from the biblical book of Proverbs, which may bring us nearer to the first Christians' confession of Jesus' origin. Proverbs contains several hundred short sayings about human life, about what people must do and how they must live to be happy; in the first chapters there are rather more extensive discussions of how you can find happiness by directing your life in accordance with wisdom. Wisdom, or the art of living, is of the utmost importance for all men. In some passages, Wisdom herself begins to speak and to give her instructions to men. In chapter 8 she goes on to describe how she was already with God before he created the universe. I read a few lines from that poetic passage.

Yahweh created me at the beginning of his work, the first of his acts of old. Ages ago I was set up, before the beginning of the earth. When there were no depths I was brought forth, when there were no springs abounding with water. Before the mountains had been shaped, before the hills, I was brought forth... When he established the heavens, I was there... When he assigned to the sea its limit, so that the waters might not transgress his command, when he marked out the foundations of the earth, I was beside him like a master workman; and I was daily his delight, rejoicing before him always, rejoicing in his inhabited world and delighting in the sons of men.

The wisdom for living which is taught in the book of Proverbs is of fundamental importance for the happiness and the joy of human beings. That is the conviction which this poet seems to be expressing, so he sees this wisdom as being produced before creation and being involved in that work of creation. In the translation above, Wisdom calls herself 'master workman', but it is far from certain that this is what the Hebrew word means. Other translators prefer 'favourite child' or 'darling'. It is also striking that Wisdom finds her delight in the human race, without any qualifications. This orientation on humanity is characteristic of the whole book of Proverbs. It never mentions the name Israel except in the title and it says nothing about themes like the Exodus, Sinai, the covenant, election, Sion and so on. It was probably completed during the fifth century BC.

At that time the Jews were beginning to separate themselves increasingly from the non-Jews among whom they lived, in order to be able to preserve their exceptional experience of faith. Round about 400 the great scribe Ezra gave clear form to that attempt by making a sacred text, the law of Moses, the Torah, the basis of Jewish society. From that time it became increasingly clear to Jews that, in distinction to other nations, they now no longer needed general rules of behaviour, which expressed the experiences of earlier generations. No, for them all wisdom was summed up in the Torah. You can find this conviction expressed very clearly in a book of the same genre as Proverbs, but written much later, round about the year 200 BC. In chapter 24 of his book, the author, known under the name of Jesus son of Sirach, also makes Lady Wisdom speak. Like the figure in the poem in Proverbs 8 she declares that she came forth from God before all things and was with him when he made the universe, the heavens and the earth and all peoples who dwell on it. Then she says that she went to seek a resting-place among men and that the Creator finally assigned to her a place where she was to go and dwell, namely Jerusalem. Then she describes how important she is for Jewish people as the source of life and happiness, and after that, in conclusion the author himself says that this woman represents the Torah. She is as it were the book-become-wisdom of God. What he wanted to say to his readers here was something like this. Do not come under the influence of the wisdom of the Greeks whose culture now also has our country in its grasp. Leave these famous philosophers alone, for our wisdom is the Torah, which is much older and comes directly from God himself.

This was the belief and the conviction of pious Jews in the time of Jesus: the Torah existed before all things with God. They also thought of that in very concrete terms. In the creation story with which the Bible begins, to begin with God creates things by himself, but when he has made the animals on the sixth day he says: 'Let us now make men...' Hence the question, 'Was there someone with him at that time to whom he could say that?' 'Yes,' was the answer of the scribes, 'he said that to the Torah.' In these circles it was also said that God created everything 'for the sake of the Torah', and the Torah is even seen as the instrument of creation: the world was created by it.

That sounds strange to us: a text, a book, which was already produced by God before creation and which was at the same time spoken of as a person. This was a remarkable way of thinking, but the conviction behind it seems to be quite clear: God has spoken and laid down for all time in the Torah his purpose for this universe and this human world, and for the people that he has chosen. There he has described how he has redeemed them and led them, and how he wishes that people to serve him. In our discussion group we had already talked a great deal about Jesus and his preaching. How he was sent by his Father who loves all men unconditionally and wants all of them to be happy, how he is concerned with his 'kingdom'. Jesus knew this will of God from the inside and he preached it passionately. In so doing he left the Torah aside and sometimes even went against its clear precepts. Whenever he spoke in his popular way about God and his kingdom and the new relationships among men and women that would come about under the rule of his God, simple people felt that this man must be right. It was all so attractive and clear, so right. No scholarship was involved, no knowledge of biblical texts. What he said came from his heart. And above all, he practised what he preached. More educated Jews saw clearly that with his freedom towards the Torah Jesus was undermining the community of faith. Leaders in positions of responsibility could not in all conscience do anything but rid the community of this false teacher.

When we came to the appearances of Jesus after his death I made only one point: of course each of the disciples assimilated these experiences, which made a very deep impression, in his own way, depending on temperament and education. Doubtless they had also talked about them together and exchanged their impressions. Soon they also did this with other Jews who had joined them, and who therefore accepted that Jesus was alive, that he had been raised by God from the dead, on the basis of their witness. In this growing group there were those who had thought through their Jewish religion more profoundly than the disciples, who had a more practical bent. These others worked things out in more 'theological' terms. Jesus had shown in all kinds of ways that he knew what God wanted from his people and for his people. Jesus had not deduced this from the Torah but seemed to know it directly, just as a beloved son senses the feelings of his father. Because by doing this he was undermining the authority of the Torah, according to a rule of that same law he was utterly rejected from the community.

For these Jewish disciples of Jesus, his appearances after his death meant that God had taken Jesus into his presence and had thus confirmed all that Jesus had said and done, including his way of showing that he knew the will of God better than the Torah.

According to Jewish belief, this 'instruction' (which is what Torah means) had already been communicated and laid down by God before the creation of the world. Now, God had endorsed Jesus, so it was clear that the Torah could not be the definitive word of God.

In other words, Jesus was even more original, even closer to what God really wanted. He had spoken, as it were, directly from God's heart. But in that case you could say more truly of Jesus what the Jewish thinkers about the Torah had said: the whole world has been created for his sake, for him and through him. Jesus was more than a sacred text with divine words which had been set down before all the ages. As a living person he was the one word in whom God had always already expressed his deepest self.

Perhaps that may sound rather strange to you, but please be patient a little longer: I'm trying to show how faith in 'the divinity of Christ' could arise within the framework of biblical thought. I could again quote Old Testament texts to illustrate what I'm saying now: the Jews were fond of seeing the activities of God in his world as a consequence of what he said. First of all there was creation itself. That came into being through the word of God, for example, 'Let there be light', and so on. He called everything, including human beings, into existence by speaking. That is also what he had done in this long history with his people. He gave his words to Moses and the prophets, but he also spoke by intervening in events; according to the Jewish way of thinking he sometimes did that by 'sending his word', as the author of Ps.107, for example, puts it (see v.20). Now all this speaking by God had come to an unsurpassable climax in the person of Jesus. God had expressed himself totally in this man. That is the reason, for example, for the confession that the word which was eternally with God had been made flesh in Jesus, a biblical expression for becoming man. Another way of putting it was to say that in Jesus God sent his only Son to us, the deepest and most authentic expression of himself.

This belief, this conviction, was expressed in the New Testament in all kinds of ways. I find one of the most impressive of them to be the first lines of the 'letter' to the Hebrews. You can never forget these lines once you've read them:

> In many and various ways God spoke of old to our fathers by the prophets; but in these last days he has spoken to us by a Son, whom he appointed the heir of all things, through whom he created the world.

That was a long monologue. So I decided to continue with a discussion. One of the women intervened. She is the mother of five children; the oldest of them can't make anything of Christian belief. She said, 'I always have difficulties over the way in which you praise Jesus so extravagantly. Plenty of other people have championed the cause of their oppressed fellow human beings and risked death for it. For example, take Martin Luther King and Bishop Oscar Romero. They were Christians, you say, who lived by their Christian faith. Granted. But non-Christians, too, may have lived like Jesus, people about whom we are completely ignorant. That may well be the case!'

Yes, it certainly may. But whether such a person can become known to a wide circle and therefore can become highly significant for others depends on the circumstances in which he or she lives such an exceptional life. In the case of Jesus two circumstances were indissolubly bound up with his history. First, he belonged to the Jewish people, dispersed over the world and quite unique by virtue of their confession of one God, origin and foundation of all that exists. This God was unique, too, in his otherness. For Jews, the only way in which they could express their bond with this God, the only one whom they recognized, was to live apart from other people, 'idolaters'. But this practice of living out their bond with him had developed in such a way that by the time of Jesus there was apartheid even in Judaism itself, at least in Palestine, on the basis of the Torah. The Jews who were obedient to all its 613 laws looked down with contempt on people who did not, the sinners and the unclean, and excluded them from the covenant; in their view these people had no access to God and no future with him. It was in this situation that Jesus appeared, with his sense of God's love for all people, his unconditional concern for all people. I call Jesus an explosion of humanity. If you put a pile of gunpowder in the street and set light to it, it bursts into flame but doesn't explode. You only get an explosion if you put the gunpowder in a container, a shell, so that it meets with resistance. The love of Jesus for men and women exploded so powerfully precisely because of this resistance in his milieu. Perhaps that's a silly comparison, but I've used it to make my first point clearly, that what happened with Jesus took place in these particular historical circumstances. There may well have been people in other times and other places who dedicated themselves totally, even sacrificed themselves, for the well-being of their fellow men and women. However, in their case the circumstances were not such that these people became so widely known throughout the world. Nor did they have the framework of Jewish thought, with its one universal God, Creator of the world and of mankind, which made it possible to attach this universal significance to the career and the person of Jesus.

The second circumstance seems to me to be this: the group of those whom Jesus chose to be his intimate disciples and who were allowed to experience after his death, in the resurrection appearances, that he was alive, is also part of the historical particularity of Jesus. The experience of this group made them certain that the one God had expressed himself definitively in the person of Jesus, in whom he had revealed his innermost being. Only they had this direct experience. We all depend on their witness. It has been carried further, handed down, over the centuries; that is what the 'church' really is. In that case you have to say that it is the Spirit of God in the hearts of believers which confirms that witness. But that's another matter.

I don't know whether or not my questioner was satisfied with this, because someone else interrupted, the engineer, who had seen the creed as a kind of invention by the church. My account of Jewish thought in connection with Jesus had been very interesting, he said, but what was so important about confessing the deity of Christ? He inspires us, after all, because he is the ideal man, that is, he is a model for us by being human. That last point is certainly a good one, and I can wholly subscribe to it. But even if we say that Jesus is the most human man who ever lived and go on to add that this is because he experienced God as the Father of all men and women, we have still not got to the point of what the creed is really trying to say. That rests on two things which I think must be taken into account. First, what you might call Jesus' claim. He declared that in his words and actions 'the kingdom of God' had come among men, and we know what he meant by this term: a love of God for men and women which gave and forgave unconditionally, a love which according to Jesus would overcome every obstacle. He himself was filled with it and was motivated by it, and as a result he became a new and effective factor in our history.

The second thing which must be taken into account is the resurrection. Jesus had remained faithful to his dedication, his obedience to God and his unconditional solidarity with men and women, even when he was tortured to death. After his death, this dead man was experienced as the living one, so that his claim was established once and for all. What the first Christians wanted to say by calling him the word made flesh, the beloved son of God, is that this revelation, this intervention of God in our history, is definitive, irrevocable, because God so to speak invested himself in Jesus. All previous revelations had the limitations of anything that happens in our history and could be supplanted by another divine intervention. In the man Jesus, God himself is present: he has as it were connected this piece of creation to his uncreated being.

I'm struggling for words here. It is clear to me what this confession of the divinity of Christ means for our daily life. By it we acknowledge that in Jesus of Nazareth, his life, proclamation, death and resurrection, God has promised us his love, his forgiveness, in fact his own life, and that this promise is unconditional and irrevocable; it cannot be taken back again. That is really the case. We may live on the basis of this certainty and continually derive hope from it despite everything that happens to us, even pain and apparently meaningless suffering, our suffering and that of people around us, despite all the doubts which overcome us and despite all scepticism. This hope is constantly revived, above all when we experience this reality together and can join in heartfelt cries like those of Paul: 'If God is for us, who or what can be against us!'

That evening we stopped there. The next time we discussed a few more points. First of all the way in which that faith in the divinity of Jesus coloured recollections of him. On a piece of paper I drew three conceptions of his career which you can find in the New Testament: The first is this:

exalted to be Messiah and Lord

earthly life

This is how Peter describes the life of Jesus in Acts 10: the story begins with his appearance in Galilee and continues after his death on a higher plane, that of Lord and Messiah, the judge of living and dead. Afterwards, another conception arose:

with God   exalted
- - - - -   - - - - - -
descent

        earthly life

Jesus descends from a higher plane, that of equality with God, by taking human existence; afterwards he was exalted to the level of God. I once called that the model of 'humiliation', as it was put into words by Paul in his letter to the Philippians.

Finally there was this pattern:

with God   exalted

‖‖‖‖‖|||||||||‖‖‖
     earthly life

The eternal word of God becomes man on earth, but at the same time remains on that divine level. The author of the Fourth Gospel seems to have had this conception in mind. In that Gospel Jesus often speaks on the basis of his union with God. Two of his miracles, that of the wine in Cana and the raising of Lazarus, demonstrate that Jesus has the creative power of God at his disposal.

So the Gospel of John above all contributed to the image of a man who is at the same time God, and this tends to make people think of omnipotence and omniscience. This Christ, God and man, could be assigned a position of power, like a ruler, in the style of the Roman emperor. And the 'deputy' of this Christ could be recognized as the head of a powerful organization.

We older Roman Catholics remembered with some amusement how we used to speak in our youth. In religious lessons and discussions people always talked about Christ, Christ who had founded the church and had instituted the sacraments and the hierarchy, with the Pope at its head as his representative, his 'deputy' on earth. The name of Jesus was reserved for piety and personal devotion, for example with 'the sacred heart of Jesus'. And we had learned always to bow our heads when we uttered the name of Jesus. It would never occur to us to call the Pope the 'deputy' of *Jesus*!

Even now we would not do that, but for other reasons. Since the historical figure of Jesus has emerged more clearly, this name has come to denote the man from Nazareth, who was called Jeshua or Jeshu by his parents, as were many other Jewish children. As a grown man who proclaimed the kingdom of God, he had an abhorrence of anything to do with power and veneration. He became cross whenever anyone revered him or even spoke deferentially to him as 'good master'. In this world, he said, there are rulers who make their subjects well aware of their power; you are not to be like that. Any one of you who wants to be great can become so only by serving others. That's what

Jesus himself did. He served his disciples at table. So he also regarded the death which was the price of his proclamation of that kingdom of God in the same way: as total service.

In the light of this picture of Jesus we cannot see the powerful Pope in Rome as his 'deputy'. Not unless he is a man who rejects any form of reverence and refuses, to use Jesus' words, to make his subjects aware of his power. Not unless he treats his fellow men with respect and trust, so that in him we recognize something of Jesus.

Perhaps that picture of Jesus may also influence the way in which we fill out the word God. If we really mean that something of the character, the attitude of God is revealed in Jesus' way of dealing with people, we cannot just go on talking of him as the 'Almighty' in the obvious sense of that word, without a little more thought. For the characteristic thing about Jesus was that he never used power, in the sense that he never compelled anyone. He tried not to browbeat people with the force of arguments, and always refused to give 'a sign from heaven' which might bring them to their knees. He often appealed to their common sense. He used his parables to make them think and to look and behave in a new way. So they always began or ended with questions: What do you think? What would you do? His preaching was challenging, alluring, in order to bring out the possibilities deep down in people. There are believing scientists who imagine the creative work of God in this way. He lured the primal matter to realize the possibilities which he had placed in it. Although these possibilities were infinitely great, and chance played an enormous part in the process, these scientists believe that we can nevertheless talk in terms of 'choices', and do so in connection with a creative will.

Even if that area is unknown ground to us, as it is to me, it seems to me to be a responsible thing, in the light of the picture of Jesus that I have sketched out, to put question marks against all the texts from the Bible and the liturgy which speak of the omnipotence of God in a way which does not wholly fit in with what Jesus shows us. Of him we say and sing that he is the image of God, the Son, and his disciple John wrote on the basis of his experience of him that God *is* love.

7 Reading in John

Recently I had a request from a 'life group' to go to explain something about the Gospel of John to them. They had chosen it as the text at their weekly celebrations for this year, but very often they couldn't make much of it. They found that the atmosphere of the Gospel was very different from the three others. A whole variety of colourful figures appear in the others, and Jesus alludes to that variegated scene whenever he talks, very directly, about the kingdom of God, with short and powerful illustrations and parables. In John Jesus usually speaks to 'the Jews', who do not really stand out very clearly. He constantly argues with them in a complicated way and at great length, and as he does so he mostly talks about himself, something that he rarely does in the other three Gospels.

He also keeps rebuking the Jews for not believing. This makes him seem strict, sometimes very harsh, and not at all sympathetic. Of course he shows himself to be warm and concerned when he is speaking with his disciples at the last supper. But even then, he is very negative when he talks about the world outside this circle.

The evening that I was to visit the group they had just read a passage from John 6 in their liturgy, about Jesus and the bread from heaven. I noted a few comments which people made about it. 'He asks a great deal of his audience.' 'It's very abstract, condensed, heavy.' Another person said, 'If you believe in me you won't be hungry again. Just imagine that!' A student remarked:'Jesus seems to be saying: You Jews are useless; I keep repeating the same thing but you don't take it in; I've already said time and again that I'm the one.' Another one said: 'It's not clear how you come to believe.' The leader of the group commented: 'Yes, Jesus did not lose anything that the Father had given him. I see this aimed at all the waste in our time. What the Emmaus communities do is a good thing; they collect together all those cast off things that get thrown away and make money out of them to give to the poor.' Someone else said: 'I can't make head or tail of that last day he keeps talking about.'

They agreed to my suggestion that I should first tell them something about the background and author of the Gospel and then try to explain to them this fragment from chapter 6 that they had read.

I began with a chart like the one on p.25 of this book. John was down at the bottom, in the 90s of our era. What happened in Palestine in the year 70 and afterwards is very important for a good understanding of his Gospel. After a long period of occupation by the Roman armies, Jerusalem was destroyed in the year 70, along with the temple which for so long had been the centre of Jewish life. At the same time the great variety of parties, groups and sects which had been so characteristic of Jewish society also vanished from the scene. Only the strongest party, the Pharisees, survived the disaster. It consisted of several thousand very dedicated people who had devoted their lives to complete and uncompromising faithfulness to God and his word, without compromise. They were real 'devotees' who formed a model group, the ideal of which was to show other Jews how an authentic Israel should live and to encourage them to do the same. Theirs was a strong group which at all events was admired by many people. The leaders of the Pharisees had already dissociated themselves from the fanatical nationalists at the time of the siege of the capital. One of them, Johanan ben Zakkai, succeeded in escaping from the city by hiding in a coffin. The Romans respected religious customs, like the burial of the dead outside the city walls. Johanan sought contact with the commander and secured his assent to found a kind of training school for Judaism at a place called Jabneh or, in Greek, Jamnia. From there he and other leaders began to organize Jewish life again after the fall of Jerusalem. They wanted to make the law of God the real centre of Jewish life, in place of the old centre which had been demolished and was no longer accessible to Jews. This was the law of God which had to be observed in the style of the Pharisees and was to be interpreted in the light of the new circumstances. Other views and life-styles could no longer be tolerated. Jews who went on observing them had to be expelled from the community of faith.

Among these outcast Jews were also those who had accepted Jesus of Nazareth as the long-expected Messiah, in Greek the Christ. It seems that at this time, in the 80s, a sentence was added to the old prayer known as the Eighteen Benedictions. This prayer consisted of a series of eighteen blessings in which the Jew expressed his dedication to God and his kingdom and his desire to bring it to pass. A further blessing was added which was in fact a curse and which must have run something like this: 'For the apostates may there be no hope, and may the Nazarenes and the heretics suddenly perish. May they be wiped out of the book of life.' Simply by virtue of the fact that this prayer also had a fixed place in the liturgy of the synagogue, it was impossible for Christian Jews to take part in that liturgy any more. They were probably also excluded from social life, and that could have economic consequences for them, for instance if people did not want to have any more dealings with them, or refused to teach a profession to their sons.

If we assume that the Gospel of John came into being among a group of such outcast Jews, then some of the texts in it begin to speak to us more clearly. That would be all the more the case if it is true, as has been recently supposed, that these groups lived in the area to the east of the Sea of Galilee. During these years it was ruled over by King Agrippa II. This grandson of Herod the Great had been granted his kingdom by the Romans and was dependent on them, but at the same time he did his best to encourage Jewish life in his territories. He maintained good relationships with the leading Pharisaic families, who could count on his help in carrying through new regulations. This was one more reason for the group of 'dissidents' to feel themselves surrounded by a hostile world and to live in constant 'fear of the Jews'. This localization in an area in the East of Palestine could also explain why the Gospel of John is so distinct, as though the milieu in which it arose stood somewhat apart from the stream of tradition on which the other three Gospels drew.

However, the real character of the work is determined above all by the person of the writer. The Christian tradition very quickly began to call him John. However, we must discover the kind of person he was from the work itself. From that it emerges that he must have been an educated Jew. Although he also spoke Greek, he knew Jewish teaching through and through. He was completely at home in the Bible and in the ways in which its texts were interpreted and applied; he knew Jewish customs and was also aware of the significance which pious Jews attached to the great feasts. It further emerges that his way of thinking is characterized by a predilection for contrasts, like truth/lie, life/death, heaven/earth, above/below, belief/unbelief. We should say that he thought in black and white, without any grey in between.

John had a very intense personal relationship with the risen Jesus, but at the same time he had reflected endlessly on the mystery of his person. As a Jew he knew from inside the many objections which could be advanced from Jewish tradition against the belief that the man from Nazareth could be the expected Messiah, doubts with which John himself had perhaps wrestled at one time. Must the Messiah not come from the family of David, from Bethlehem? He was expected to know the law of God better than the ordinary scribes and be completely obedient to it. He would see through people, look into their hearts, and there would be no end to his reign. This Jesus who had appeared as a teacher about fifty years before did not come from Bethlehem in Judah, but from the little village of Nazareth, in Galilee of all places. He soon met his end, crucified by the Roman governor. And rightly so. For he had openly transgressed the law of God and had put his own authority above that of the law, a horrific piece of presumption. Finally, and most important of all, with the coming of the Messiah everything was expected to change; after he had condemned and destroyed all the wicked he was going to give life a new dimension – and Jesus had done none of these things.

These were the great questions which John particularly wanted to discuss in his book. It is not certain whether he knew the other three Gospels. In any case he was familiar with the genre which Mark had begun: a description of Jesus' public activity from the time of his baptism in the Jordan, then his suffering, his crucifixion and the appearances which followed. That was the plan that he chose for his work, in which he wanted to strengthen belief in Jesus the Messiah and Son of God among his fellow Jewish Christians by arming them against the difficulties which the Jewish world had begun to present to them. In their difficult circumstances some of them will have felt the temptation to leave the community of Christ and return to the safe old home of the synagogue.

In passing, I should point out that there must have been another possibility for them. They could have joined the movement or sect which had come into being around John the Baptist in which he was revered as the Messiah. At that time this group must have still have had its attractions for people whom the evangelist knew. More than once in his story he explicitly makes John the Baptist say that he himself is not the Messiah, and that his task is only to go before him and bear witness to him.

But that was just an incidental matter. For the evangelist is chiefly concerned with the relationship between faith in Jesus as he himself experienced it and proclaimed it and its rejection by the Jews of his time, the Pharisees. That is the main subject of the long conversations which he makes Jesus have with 'the Jews'. These are in fact discussions between John and the Jewish tradition which he knows from the inside, and probably also discussions between him and representatives of it. For it sometimes seems that thinking Jews were impressed by this group of Jesus-people and their leader John, and that they sought opportunities to talk with them. That was difficult. They could not visit these outcasts in public, since in that case they too ran the risk of being counted as heretics. In chapter 3, John describes how the learned Nicodemus, the teacher of Israel, who was foremost among the Jews, came to talk with Jesus (i.e. with the Christians) by night (i.e. secretly). In chapter 12 we find: 'Nevertheless many even of the authorities believed in him, but for fear of the Pharisees they did not confess it, lest they should be put out of the synagogue.'

This situation is also clear in the brilliantly told story in John 9, about the man born blind. When this man has been healed by Jesus, he is brought to 'the Pharisees', and later the writer refers to this same group as 'the Jews'. They summon his parents, but can't get anything out of them. For these parents, we read, 'feared the Jews, for the Jews had already agreed that if any one should confess him to be Christ, he was to be put out of the synagogue.' When the man who was healed later goes on to say that someone who can open the eyes of a man born blind must come from God, 'the Jews' get cross, call him a sinner and throw him out of the synagogue. When he next meets Jesus, he comes to believe in him as the Son of man. This is an old title for Jesus which John prefers to use to show him as the one who has descended from heaven in order to bring God's salvation into this world. The blind man who is healed is really healed by beginning to 'see' Jesus. He becomes a Christian. The story ends with a harsh word to the Pharisees, who refuse to arrive at this 'seeing' and persist in their sin, that is, their blindness, their unbelief. It is typical of John to construct such a dramatic story with the aid of the two senses of being blind and seeing.

So this is real biblical history writing: past and present are as it were fused together. John describes that piece of the past from the 30s, when Jesus of Nazareth was at work, in terms of his own day, in the 90s, when he and his community are confronted with Pharisaic Judaism. And he does so by giving a radically different answer to the question who Jesus was: the Messiah sent by God or an impostor, a sinner. The latter is what the Pharisees, the Jews, said to the man who was healed of his blindness. We know that this man is a sinner. He replies mockingly to their question whether he will tell them how Jesus opened his eyes. 'Do you want to become his disciples, too?' To which they retort scornfully: 'You are a disciple of this man and we are disciples of Moses. We know that God has spoken to Moses, but we do not know where this man comes from.' It is striking that in his reply, the man who has been healed responds in the plural. 'We know that God does not listen to sinners...' Here he is speaking in the name of the Christian community. Whereas Judaism in these years after 70 began to base itself on 'Moses', i.e. the law, the revelation of God, Christians believe that in Jesus God has brought a new definitive revelation of himself and his love, his salvation. That salvation is present and at work in the person of Jesus. He *is* this revelation in person.

In the style of this kind of history writing John makes Jesus say this himself, especially in the often repeated 'I am'. Sometimes he just says 'I am', and no more; more often he adds something else, as in chapter 6: 'I am the bread of life', and: 'I am the living bread that has come down from heaven'. This way of talking about himself and introducing himself did not go down well in the reading of the passage. Therefore it is worth while pointing out that the people who accompanied Jesus never heard him speak in this way. On the contrary. It struck them that he always avoided this. When John the Baptist sent from prison to ask Jesus, 'Are you the one who is to come or have we to look for another?', the answer was not, 'Go and tell John that I am,' but, 'Go and tell him what is happening, that the blind see, the lame walk, lepers are cleansed, the deaf hear, the dead are raised, and the poor have the good news preached to them.' And another example: Jesus once recalled the story about King Solomon: a queen from the distant south came all the way to Jerusalem to hear the wisdom of Solomon; at the last judgment she will bear witness against the people of this generation, for 'here is something more than Solomon'. He does not say, 'I am more than Solomon.'

At the same time Jesus amazed people by 'speaking with authority', as they put it. He seems to have been very certain about what God wanted and did not refer in this connection to the divine revelation set down in the law of Moses. He knew that from within, from his striking familiarity with the God of Israel whom he addressed with that term of childlike trust, Abba, rather like our 'Dad'. No Jew had ever dared to address God in this way.

In the years after Easter the disciples began to realize what had been the deepest ground of Jesus' familiarity with God, its deepest roots. The one who had 'appeared' to them after his death, from the divine sphere into which he had evidently been taken up, must also have come down from there. So for him, dying was 'a return to the Father' from whom he had come forth. As John put it in the profound foreword to his Gospel: the Word in which God expressed himself completely, outside all time, has been 'made flesh' in the person of Jesus, a historical man among other men.

John is very fond of using the word 'send' to describe the mysterious transition from God's timeless world above to our own: Jesus is 'sent' by the Father into the world. More specifically than in our society, in ancient biblical stories the one who is sent, for example by a king, is seen and treated much more as the one whom he represents (literally, 'makes present'), and the one who is sent only announces what he has been instructed to. Now Jesus represents God, the God who revealed himself to Moses as the saviour and liberator of Israel. In this role he spoke of himself as 'I am' in an active, dynamic sense: I am involved, I am here among you to save you. This way in which God makes himself known is certainly in John's mind when at serious moments he makes Jesus say, 'I am'. For example, chapter 8 ends with the solemn declaration, 'Before Abraham was, I am.' Understandably, the writer adds a comment: 'Then the Jews took up stones to stone him.' Understandably, since in this saying Jesus claimed for himself a role which belonged only to God, and for Jews that was intolerable.

When something else comes after that 'I am', it always relates to the complete salvation that God brings in Jesus, the salvation of which Jesus is the personal embodiment. He *is* the bread that will satisfy our human hunger: he *is* the light that drives away the darkness in which we live; he *is* the resurrection from the death that constantly has us in its grasp; he *is* the way to God which is the fullness of life, the truth.

Pious Jews used some of these images to express what the Torah meant for them as a revelation of God's will: it was a light on their path, nourishment on their way to God. It may be that John also wanted to say this: for us, salvation is now no longer embodied in the Torah, but in Jesus. But at the same time these are terms which people everywhere use as figurative expressions of their deepest hopes and longings.

Incidentally, I should point out that the Christians for whom John wrote his Gospel had fewer difficulties with the 'I am' style than we do. For at that time a number of preachers were travelling round Syria and Palestine who had come from the East and on the basis of a special 'illumination' claimed that they came from God, or were themselves gods come to earth to offer people eternal salvation. Anyone who did not listen to them would perish. According to texts which have been preserved from that milieu, the 'I' style was quite usual among these preachers.

But perhaps this comment is superfluous. For it could be that the Christians who had already had John as their inspired leader for years had been made familiar with the 'I' style by him. In moments of exaltation he could address his people in the name of Jesus, as though Jesus himself were speaking. At those times the spirit which Jesus had sent after his departure to replace him was speaking through him. This Spirit would make clear what he had really meant. Chapters 13-17 in this Gospel are chiefly about this, and are dedicated to the conversations which Jesus had with his disciples during their last meal together.

Now let's discuss that part of chapter 6.

'Truly, truly, I say to you, you seek me, not because you saw signs, but because you ate your fill of the loaves. Do not labour for the food which perishes, but for the food which endures to eternal life, which the Son of man will give to you, for on him God has set his seal.' Then they said to him, 'What must we do, to be doing the work of God?' Jesus answered them, 'This is the work of God, that you believe in him whom he has sent.' So they said to him, 'Then what sign do you do, that we may see, and believe you? What miracle do you perform? Our fathers ate the manna in the wilderness; as it is written, "he gave them bread from heaven to eat."' Jesus then said to them, 'Truly, truly, I say to you, it was not Moses who gave you the bread from heaven; my Father gives you the true bread from heaven. For the bread of God is that which comes down from heaven, and gives life to the world.' They said to him, 'Give us this bread always.'

Jesus said to them, 'I am the bread of life; he who comes to me shall not hunger and he who believes in me shall never thirst. But I said to you that you have seen me and yet do not believe. All that the Father gives me will come to me and him who comes to me I will not cast out. For I have come down from heaven, not to do my own will, but the will of him who sent me; and this is the will of him who sent me, that I should lose nothing of all that he has given me but raise it up at the last day. For this is the will of my Father, that everyone who sees the Son and believes in him should have eternal life; and I will raise him up at the last day.'

The Jews then murmured at him because he said, 'I am the bread which came down from heaven.' They said, 'Is this not Jesus, the son of Joseph, whose father and mother we know? How does he now say, "I have come down from heaven?"' Jesus answered them, 'Do not murmur among yourselves. No one can come to me unless the Father who sent me draws him; and I will raise him up at the last day. It is written in the prophets, "And they shall all be taught by God". Everyone who has heard and learned from the Father comes to me. Not that any one has seen the Father except him who is from God; he has seen the Father. Truly, truly I say to you, he who believes has eternal life.'

This passage is the first part of a typical 'discourse' of Jesus, following the story of a miracle, a 'sign', as in the previous chapter. In this case the sign is twofold. First, Jesus satisfied a great crowd of people with five loaves and two fishes; then the night afterwards he went on foot over the raging waters of the lake, to the boat in which he had sent his disciples to the other side. The story of these two miracles also occurs in Mark 6, and there too there is already a link between the two. For Mark describes how the disciples were beside themselves when Jesus came to them in such a mysterious way and got into their boat. He gives as the reason for this amazement the fact that they had not understood the miracle of the loaves because 'their heart was hardened', a biblical way of saying that their understanding, their insight, was inhibited. Mark seems to want to say that they had understood this miraculous feeding only in the material sense, perhaps even as a kind of 'messianic' wonder, a repetition of what God had done for his people in the wilderness: they were fed with manna. But what the people had not understood was the new way in which God had come near to them in Jesus. His nocturnal appearance was meant to make that clear to them.

Whether John had once read this story in Mark or knew it from another source, at all events he tells the two miracles in his own style and with new details. And above all, he goes much more thoroughly than Mark into its significance as a revelation of what Jesus means to be for us men and women in the deepest sense. One of these new details is that the people who were fed were so excited that they wanted to make Jesus king, i.e. to hail him as Messiah, and that he therefore went away from them to a solitary place. Then John makes these Galilean people, who knew nothing of Jesus' nocturnal journey over the water, go to seek Jesus the next day and ask him, 'Rabbi, when did you come here?' In this way John has set the scene for Jesus to talk to people about himself.

He begins with a solemn answer to their question.

> Truly, truly, I say to you, you seek me, not because you saw signs, but because you ate your fill of the loaves.

They had understood the feeding as a messianic miracle, but John says that that was a misconception. Jesus meant this feeding to be a token of the real, authentic food that he wanted to give to people. Indeed, this is what he himself wanted to be for them. But that was only possible if they exerted themselves, 'laboured' for it.

> Do not labour for the food which perishes, but for the food which endures to eternal life, which the Son of man will give to you, for on him God has set his seal.

Only God can give the food that quenches man's deepest hunger, his longing for unbounded fullness of life. And he seeks to do that through Jesus, the Son of man to whom he has given this power, just as the written declaration of a ruler only has validity when he has set his personal seal on it.

> Then they said to him, 'What must we do, to be doing the work of God?' Jesus answered them, 'This is the work of God, that you believe in him whom he has sent.'

As good Jews, people ask about the works, the many actions, that they have to do or not do in order to respond to the will of God. But now the same God requires only one work, one deed: to believe in Jesus, the one whom he has sent by God. They want to do that, but first Jesus must do something, give a sign which legitimates him.

> So they said to him, 'Then what sign do you do, that we may see, and believe you? What miracle do you perform? Our fathers ate the manna in the wilderness; as it is written, "he gave them bread from heaven to eat."'

Jesus ought to be doing something identical to the miracle with the manna in the wilderness. That miracle of God's daily care for his people was often recalled and celebrated in the Bible. From these texts, John chooses a verse from Psalm 78, because in it the manna is called 'bread from heaven'. Remember that in

Greek the word 'bread' is masculine: people can talk about what bread does as what a 'he' does, comes down and gives life.

> Jesus then said to them, 'Truly, truly, I say to you, it was not Moses who gave you the bread from heaven; my father gives you the true bread from heaven. For the bread of God is that which comes down from heaven, and gives life to the world.'

It is part of John's style, his technique of writing, to make the conversation-partners of Jesus ask questions which rest on a misunderstanding. They interpret a saying of Jesus on a different level from that on which he is thinking. In this way John gives Jesus the opportunity of expressing himself more clearly.

> They said to him, 'Give us this bread always.' Jesus said to them, 'I am the bread of life; he who comes to me shall not hunger and he who believes in me shall never thirst.'

John has worked out the whole of the previous discussion to culminate in this 'word' of revelation: Jesus is the one who fulfils the primal human need for unbounded life and happiness, who brings that for which every person hungers and thirsts most deeply. These two needs of life belong together, though hitherto the conversation has been only about bread that satisfies hunger. In biblical prayers the desire to be close to God is often expressed with the word 'thirst', a thirst for life, for community with the living God. By using these two terms, hunger and thirst, which express the same longing, John can connect two other terms which have the same content for him: 'come to Jesus' and 'believe in Jesus'.

These terms play a part in the next passage, a piece of John's 'theology' in which they are connected with other important themes, like the complete unity of will between Jesus and the Father, and that will is concerned with human salvation. For John the Christian community consists of those who have been given to him by the Father, who have been drawn to him by the Father. They have seen Jesus in the same way as the other Jews; but these did not come to see him in the deeper sense of believing: seeing him as the Son of Man who comes from God. Those who came to Jesus did see him in that way. Because of that they now already have a share in the divine life that Jesus gives, and will be certain of their resurrection on the last day.

But I said to you that you have seen me and yet do not believe. All that the Father gives me will come to me and him who comes to me I will not cast out. For I have come down from heaven, not to do my own will, but the will of him who sent me; and this is the will of him who sent me, that I should lose nothing of all that he has given me but raise it up at the last day. For this is the will of my Father, that everyone who sees the Son and believes in him should have eternal life; and I will raise him up at the last day.

Hitherto Jesus had been talking with Galilean people who had experienced the miraculous feeding and had sought him. Jesus then says to them that they did not believe. Therefore John now goes on to refer to them as 'the Jews'. He describes how they began to 'murmur'. This term comes from the biblical narratives about the journey through the wilderness, especially the story of the manna. The people rebelled over the gracious acts with which God surrounded them at that time. They would rather have remained among the fleshpots of Egypt than be driven on by a God who wanted to liberate them because he loved his people. Although God shows such powerful initiatives in his love, people have the possibility of resisting it and even of giving reasons for doing so!

The Jews then murmured at him because he said, 'I am the bread which came down from heaven.' They said, 'Is this not Jesus, the son of Joseph, whose father and mother we know? How does he now say, "I have come down from heaven?" '

Here John is posing the greatest difficulty which was raised for Christian faith, for that belief which John tended to express more sharply than anyone else. How can an ordinary person, born and brought up among human beings, at the same time be a figure from heaven who embodies the life and salvation of God, who is the revelation of God in person? John cannot give a rational reply to this difficulty. All that he can say is that only God is in a position to help people over this threshold, by 'drawing' them to him. Perhaps here he is thinking of a saying of the prophet Hosea, who in chapter 11 describes how God loved his people and 'drew' them with cords of love. Another way by which God brings someone to believe in Jesus is by teaching this person himself. Jews can read in their Bibles, in the prophets, that God will do this. Anyone who listens carefully to this biblical instruction from God can arrive at belief in Jesus. That helps them to know God better, since only Jesus can give the full revelation of God, because he is the only one who has seen the Father.

> Jesus answered them, 'Do not murmur among yourselves. No one can come to me unless the Father who sent me draws him; and I will raise him up at the last day. It is written in the prophets, "And they shall all be taught by God." Everyone who has heard and learned from the Father comes to me. Not that any one has seen the Father except him who is from God; he has seen the Father.'

That is how I tried to explain the passage from John 6 a bit that evening. It did not resolve all the difficulties. I had not made clear how you come to faith, still less why Jesus is so hard on the Jews. I think that these questions hang together, because both of them have to do with the experiences of John and his community. Try to imagine how these people felt outcasts from the Jewish community, yet at the same time felt themselves to have been chosen to believe in Jesus the Messiah and Son of God. Most of them were doubtless born Jews. It must have been terrifying for them that the majority of their people had once rejected Jesus and now had driven them, who believed in him, so irrevocably from their midst. This strong resistance from the old faith certainly contributed to the fact that their leader John had reflected so deeply on the divine origin of Jesus. He himself felt strongly attracted by Jesus, and loved by him. The way in which he talked on the basis of this intimate relationship found such a grateful hearing in his community that their common faith in Jesus became almost self-evident, as natural as the air that they breathed. That the Jewish world outside had totally rejected this could not be explained by lack of insight and purpose; no, a supernatural factor had to be at work, a power hostile to God. Judaism had formed a clear picture of it in the last centuries before Christ and had even given it names. Satan, the devil, the prince of the demons who rule in this world. I mention this also as a preparation for what we find later in the Gospel, in chapter 8. There Jesus says to the Jews that they are not of God, because if they were they would also love Jesus. No, their father is the devil, the murderer of men and an arch-liar from the beginning. The Jews are not from God. Hence their complete rejection of Jesus, who is from God, and of those who believe in him. For they, too, are born of God.

It seems as though John is thinking of a kind of predestination. Sometimes he gives moral reasons: the Jews are seeking their own honour, their own advantage. Those who act badly, we find in chapter 3, have a hatred of the light, for fear that their deeds will be manifest in it. But those who do the truth go to the light. Thus people would determine by their behaviour whether or not they came to faith. However, the main emphasis is on their origin, whether they come from God or from the devil, the world. Therefore this Gospel nowhere tells us how we might come to faith.

The world by which the group of believers felt themselves to be surrounded and threatened in fact coincides with the Jewish community around them. John calls the devil the Father of the Jews, but also the prince of this world. This is so contrary to Jesus that John makes him say of them in his prayer in chapter 17: 'I pray for them, my disciples. I do not pray for the world but for those whom you have given me because they belong to you.' So here, too, there is an expression of complete separation. On the one hand we have Jesus, the believer, and on the other hand the world, the devil, the Jews.

Fortunately, however, John does not always carry through this thinking in absolute opposites. In chapter 3, after Jesus' conversation with Nicodemus, he introduces a few sentences which are clearly a confession of faith. Here the world is not thought of as written off: 'God so loved the world that he gave his only son to the end that all who believe in him should not perish but have eternal life.' In the prayer from chapter 17 which I quoted above, Jesus later prays to God for the mutual unity of his disciples, 'That the world may believe that you have sent me.' The world referred to here may therefore well arrive at faith. And when in chapter 12 Jesus speaks about his future 'lifting up' on the cross, he promises, 'then I shall draw all men to me' – all men, without exceptions.

In his very distinctive manner, John too proclaims the life and death of Jesus as the unsurpassable act of God's love for us men.

88

What makes reading his Gospel so difficult for us is his years of practice in what I shall call biblical meditation on the person, the work and the suffering of Jesus, which he presents in his own style: strong contrasts, the use of words on two levels of meaning, the shift from today to the past and back again – just to mention a few peculiarities.

So a good deal is asked of us if we are to let John speak to us properly. I would say that what is needed is a kind of contemplative tranquillity. A saying like 'I am the good shepherd' in chapter 10 only takes on its full significance when we have brought in a number of texts from the Old Testament, like Ezekiel 34 and Psalm 23 and, when we have experienced what it is to hear his voice calling us by name. The expression 'I am the true vine and you are the branches' could appear in John, since biblical texts about Israel as God's vineyard were combined in his mind with reminiscences of sayings of Jesus and with the reality of the living bond between Jesus and those who believe in him, which was part of his everyday experience. For all these reasons, texts from John seem heavy and condensed, as someone put it.

8 The Story of the Passion – Told Four Times

Every year, towards Easter, I am asked to talk to groups of interested people about the passion narratives in the four Gospels. In the space of one evening you can read only a few passages from them. Last year, the first piece I chose was the story of the arrest of Jesus, which is narrated by each of the four evangelists; then I went on to the words which Jesus spoke as he was hanging on the cross. As usual, I put up the chart which is printed on p.25 of this book, so that everyone could see it. I think that this is a great help in keeping us aware of how much time passed between the event itself and the written accounts of it. At the same time, we can see from it that Matthew and Luke incorporated the story which Mark had written earlier into their texts, each in his own way, and that John's approach stands somewhat apart.

After a few introductory remarks we read the passages I've mentioned. Then we had a quarter of an hour's silent meditation, and after that we discussed the thoughts and feelings that had come to us.

These introductory remarks were about the nature of the passion narratives. Deep down in many Christians is the conviction that these are historical reports, exact accounts of what could be seen and heard in Jerusalem on that Thursday and Friday. Perhaps that kind of thinking stems from the belief that because the Bible is a special book, inspired by God, it can only contain 'truth' in the sense that God himself guarantees that it contains no stories which do not faithfully reproduce the events they describe. That is to forget that this conception of the 'truth' of a story is a modern Western idea, something of which the biblical writers had no notion. When in their world a story was told about the past which had anything to do with their faith, the intention was not to hand on what precisely had happened at one particular moment in history; it was not the communication of purely historical knowledge. They were far more concerned with the meaning of what happened at the time, its significance for today, the today of the storytellers and their audiences, the writers and their readers, and they also expressed this meaning in their story.

Let me give an example: the 'today' of the first generation of Christians was governed by their certainty that in what had happened with Jesus, his death and resurrection, God had given a completely new twist to world history. That might sound pompous to anyone who is unaware that at this time many Jews were expecting such a divine act of intervention. Of course people imagined all kinds of ways in which it would come about, but believing Jews were in agreement over the essentials: their God would establish his sole rule over all the world, and so no power would be able to harm his people any more. A particular kind of imagery, and 'apocalytic' language had already been developed over a number of centuries to describe that cosmic event. This was quickly used by Christians in their story about the death of Jesus.

At mid-day on the day when he was hung on the cross to die, they said, a deep darkness fell upon all the land: a 'cosmic' sign which already had a fixed place in descriptions of the judgment that God would bring upon the evil world on 'his day'. In chapter 8 of the book of the prophet Amos, God is made to say: 'On that day I will make the sun go down at mid-day and I will darken the earth in clear daylight.' Perhaps the notice of Christians was also brought to this saying in Amos by what was said a few lines lower down in connection with it: 'mourning over an only son'. It appears from the Gospel of Matthew that another traditional cosmic sign was added to the darkness, a violent earthquake.

The Christians also told how at the moment of Jesus' death the curtain of the temple was torn down the middle. This was also a sign of the new twist which God was giving at that moment to his history with mankind. Jesus had been sent to proclaim by word and deed the new way in which God wanted to treat people in his coming kingdom. When he died, he had fulfilled this task to the end and this new way had been opened up in him. The Jewish temple and Jewish sacrificial worship had had their day as ways to God for that one people: the God of Israel, invisibly present behind the curtain of this temple, had now made himself manifest and accessible to all men in this crucified figure.

Something else determined the 'today' of the first Christians. These Jews had to explain to one another and to their fellow-Jews a quite bewildering fact: they recognized the long-awaited Saviour of humankind, the Messiah, in a man from Nazareth who had been executed as a criminal, accused of blasphemy by the supreme Jewish authorities, and put to death in a shameful manner by the Roman forces of occupation as a rebel against lawful authority. As Jews, how could they take in something like this? They found the answer to this question in the Bible. Their interest in reading their Bibles was not like that of people today; they did not ask, 'What did the biblical author mean by this text when he wrote it?' No, for them this Jewish Bible was the Word of God, and they were the people to whom it was now addressed.

One could say that they regarded the whole of scripture as a prophecy' of the climax of history, in which they themselves were involved. Everything beforehand had been written with an eye to these events. That was quite clear in some texts. For example, there were some Psalms, 22 and 69 in particular, in which the poet David describes how much he has to suffer from enemies, and how he is afflicted by pain and torture. He then goes on immediately to thank God for delivering him from all these deadly torments. It was clear that in these Psalms, David, illuminated by the Spirit, had described the future career of his great descendant, the Messiah, who was to be born from his family. The ancient scriptures also often tell of prophets who in the name of God attacked injustice, championed the poor and oppressed, and who therefore often had to undergo torture and sometimes were even killed. In this respect, too, their careers were foretastes of what would happen to the last of all the prophets.

Thus the death of Jesus had not been a matter of chance, not even a whim of fortune; it was not as if evil people had acted of their own volition. No, everything had been decided and fore-ordained by God himself. So Jesus had obediently followed the course that his Father had marked out for him in the scriptures. He was controlled, so to speak, by a divine necessity. That is expressed most clearly by Luke in his famous story of the disciples on the road to Emmaus: on the way Jesus explains to them how everything had been foreordained in the Law, the Prophets and the Psalms; then he says to them: 'Had not the Messiah to suffer all these things in order to enter into his glory!'

Lastly, I mentioned something that often influenced the situation of the Christian storytellers and their audiences: sometimes their small communities had to endure harsh experiences, above all as a result of outside opposition. Jews who could not accept the fact that they worshipped the crucified Jesus as the Messiah often did not stop short of disapproval, and made their lives difficult in all kinds of ways. That happened above all when Jewish Christians accepted non-Jews into their community. Moreover, in Gentile cities those who joined a Christian community often had to break off all kinds of social ties, and sometimes that provoked vigorous reactions. In these circumstances the story of Jesus' suffering also took on the character of a model: it encouraged people to follow him bravely on his way of humiliation and pain. Furthermore, in telling the story people also paid special attention to the disciples who had left him in the lurch and had even betrayed him. People must not deny him in the way that Peter had denied him. The story of Peter's denial is told at length. There was just as much stress on the action of Judas, who had also been one of the Twelve.

As we discuss the first fragment, the short account which describes how Jesus was arrested in the garden at the foot of the Mount of Olives called Gethsemane, i.e. 'olive press', we shall now see how each evangelist added emphases of his own when he put down in writing the often-told story.

According to Mark (14.43-52)

After his prayer in the Garden of Olives, Jesus had told his disciples to rise: 'See, my betrayer is at hand.' Mark continues:

And immediately, while he was still speaking, Judas came,

93

one of the twelve, and with him a crowd with swords and clubs, from the chief priests and the scribes and the elders. Now the betrayer had given them a sign, saying, 'The one I shall kiss is the man; seize him and lead him away safely.' And when he came, he went up to him at once, and said, 'Master', and kissed him. And they laid hands on him and seized him.

Here Mark has given a brief and compelling account of the essentials: Jesus is taken prisoner. The reader had learnt earlier that Judas, surnamed Iscariot, had planned to hand Jesus over to the Jewish authorities. The reader already knows him as 'one of the Twelve', but there was more to it than that: he was one of the Twelve who had been sitting at table with Jesus immediately beforehand and sharing bread with him. His close connection with Jesus is also indicated in the promised sign, a kiss.

Mark adds a few details to this rounded-off scene. Before we read this second part, here are some comments. One of the themes in Mark's Gospel is the failure of Jesus' disciples to understand. They do not grasp who he really is and they get very agitated whenever he talks of his future suffering. Perhaps that is why he mentions the sword stroke by one of those who were with Jesus. What Jesus then says to the crowd is really meant for those who supported these police officials. Why this secrecy, these goings on by night, when I always spoke openly in the temple and am ready to go the way marked out for me in the scriptures? Jesus is left completely alone when the disciples have fled.

Finally, Mark mentions an apparently inquisitive young man who only escapes with his life by running away naked. It has been supposed that this young man was Mark himself. In that case, this detail would be a kind of signature to his work, rather like the way in which mediaeval artists used to draw their own portraits in the corner of a paintings of crowd scenes. However, there can be another interpretation of the young man who ran away naked without his linen garment. The term 'nakedness' was sometimes used in the young churches in the sense of not being clad with courage and bravery; furthermore, it was the custom for those who were being accepted into the community to be dressed in a linen garment after they had been immersed in the water of baptism. The young man who had 'followed' Jesus and run away when there was danger might be a warning from Mark to young men who had decided to join a Christian community without thinking of the courage which following Jesus might demand. Now let's go on to read the second part of Mark's story:

> But one of those who stood by drew his sword, and struck the slave of the high priest and cut off his ear. And Jesus said to them, 'Have you come out as against a robber, with swords and clubs to capture me? Day after day I was with you in the temple teaching, and you did not seize me. But let the scriptures be fulfilled.' And they all forsook him and fled. And a young man followed him, with nothing but a linen cloth around his body; and they seized him, but he left the linen cloth and ran away naked.

According to Matthew (26.47-56)

About fifteen years later Matthew rewrote this account of the arrest of Jesus. A good deal had happened in the meantime. Jerusalem had been destroyed by the Romans in AD 70. Under the strong leadership of the Pharisees, the Jews had worked out new patterns of life and belief to help them preserve their common faith in this new situation, now that the temple was no longer their centre. Anyone who now openly confessed Jesus of Nazareth as the Messiah of Israel was 'cast out of the synagogue', as the phrase went. So the Christians in Palestine and Syria began to form separate communities which existed alongside and in opposition to the Jewish communities. The Gospel of Matthew came into being in such a group of Greek-speaking Jewish Christians. People in that group knew Mark's work, but a great many more sayings of Jesus, and some stories about him, were in circulation in this community, in both written and oral form. Hence the plan to make a new and enlarged edition of Mark.

The evangelist Matthew often expressed the awareness of his community that the Christians really made up the new and true Israel, over against the old Israel which had rejected Jesus and therefore its Messiah. Moreover, Matthew brought together many sayings of Jesus into larger complexes, almost speeches, which he inserted at five points in his Gospel, just as Moses once wrote the Law in five books. For Matthew, Jesus is the teacher and lawgiver of the new people of God. When it comes to the story of Jesus' passion, Matthew shows even more clearly than Mark that Jesus was not the victim of his enemies who could do what they wanted with him: no, as the obedient Son of God he remained in charge of events throughout. That is already clear when the passion story proper begins (in Mark 14). At that point Mark himself provides an indication of time and goes on to say that the conspiracy against Jesus had been forged: 'It was now two days before the Passover and the feast of Unleavened Bread. And the chief priests and the scribes were seeking how to arrest him by stealth, and kill him.' In Matthew 26 it is Jesus who gives the indication of time; he appears to know what is going to happen to him: 'He said to his disciples, "You know that after two days the Passover is coming, and the Son of man will be delivered up to be crucified." Then the chief priests and the elders of the people gathered. . . and took counsel together in order to arrest Jesus by stealth, and kill him.' It is as though Jesus himself sets the drama of the passion in motion with his prediction. Matthew also seems to suggest the same thing in his version of Mark's account of the arrest of Jesus. I have put his additions in italics.

> While he was still speaking, *behold*, Judas came, one of the twelve, and with him a *great* crowd with swords and clubs, from the chief priests and the elders *of the people*. Now the betrayer had given them a sign, saying, 'The one I shall kiss is the man; seize him.' And he came up to Jesus at once and said,'*Hail*, Rabbi,' and kissed him. *Jesus said to him, 'Friend, why are you here?' Then they came up*, laid hands on *Jesus* and seized him.

The interjection 'behold' or 'and behold' is a stylistic form used in the Bible to underline the importance of the story or to give it dramatic effect. The crowd is a 'great' one, the term stressing how ridiculous this display of police force is against the person to be arrested. The elders are 'of the people': that people rejects its Messiah. Matthew adds the customary greeting before the title 'Rabbi', which strikingly is used only by Judas in this Gospel.

The word 'friend' which Jesus uses to address Judas is not the Greek *philos*, which denotes true friendship and is often used by Luke and also by John. Here we have *hetairos*, something like 'mate, comrade'. It occurs in the New Testament only in Matthew, here and twice elsewhere, in stories told by Jesus. The owner of a vineyard who pays as much to the workers who arrive last as he does to those who have worked all day uses this word when he says to the spokesman of the latter group, 'Friend, I do you no wrong.' The other story is about a king who organized a wedding feast for his son and noticed among the guests a man who was not wearing a wedding garment. He said to him, 'Friend, how do you come to be here without a wedding garment?'

What comes after 'friend' is not so clear. Literally, it is 'wherefore you are here...' Many translations, like the RSV above, translate it as a question, 'Why are you here?' Perhaps, though, it is better to fill out the phrase and translate it: 'What you are here for can now happen'; in that case, as Matthew sees things, it is again Jesus who as it were gives permission to the members of the crowd to carry out their plan.

Now to the second part of the story. Matthew again presents his master as a teacher and makes him repeat once more what he had taught in his first discourse, the Sermon on the Mount. You must not respond to violence with violence, but defuse it by submitting to it. And here Jesus again adopts the attitude he took to Satan at the beginning of Matthew's Gospel: he does not want to make any use of the powers which he has at his disposal as Son of God; he seeks in obedience to follow the way of suffering which God has appointed for him in the scriptures.

Matthew introduces Jesus' address to the crowd rather more solemnly than Mark does. He knows that a teacher always sits to teach in the temple. Furthermore, he stresses that the whole of the drama of the passion must take place for the scriptures to be fulfilled, and he says more clearly than Mark that it was the disciples who all took flight.

And behold, one of those *who were with Jesus stretched out his hand* and drew his sword, and struck the slave of the high priest, and cut off his ear. *Then Jesus said to him, 'Put your sword back in its place; for all who take the sword will perish by the sword. Do you think that I cannot appeal to my Father, and he will at once send me more than twelve legions of angels? But how then should the scriptures be fulfilled, that it must be so?'* At that hour Jesus said to *the crowds*, 'Have you come out as against a robber, with swords and clubs to capture me? Day after day I *sat* in the temple teaching, and you did not seize me. But *all this has taken place* that the scriptures *of the prophets* should be fulfilled.' Then all *the disciples* forsook him and fled.

According to Luke (22.47-53)

The care with which Luke works over Mark's stories is evident from his version of this account. He finds it technically rather awkward that Mark should refer back in his story to an earlier moment when the arrangement with the kiss is made. In his version, Judas comes forward and approaches Jesus to kiss him. Luke does not give him a chance to carry out that underhand plan: Jesus already knows what his intention is. Mark says that they take Jesus captive at this stage; however, Luke seems to wonder how a manacled man can do what happens next. Note, too, that those present can only strike after they have put a question to Jesus: conversations are characteristic of Luke's stories. He adds that the ear which was cut off was the right one, and cannot imagine that Jesus, the great healer, who loved even his enemies, would have left the wound unhealed.

Luke feels that the words which Jesus says to the crowd are misplaced, since the people who had given the orders, and whom Mark mentioned, are not there in person. So he makes them appear on the scene. Jesus says that they have come out with swords and staves, but does not add, as in Mark, 'to capture me'. They cannot do that in their own strength, but only when their hour has struck, when the evil powers are given the freedom to go their way. Now Jesus seems to give them that freedom.

Finally, note that Luke does not mention the flight of the disciples. That may be in order to put them in a better light, something that he often does when he rewrites Mark. But it may also be connected with Luke's purpose. He is the only evangelist to give the Twelve the title 'apostles'. In his view, the qualification for that office is to have experienced everything from Jesus' activity in Galilee up to and including his ascension. Luke does not make the appearances of Jesus after his death take place in Galilee, like the other evangelists, but in Jerusalem. So he cannot allow the disciples to flee from the city to Galilee. Luke describes the arrest as follows:

> While he was still speaking, behold a crowd, and the man called Judas, one of the twelve, was leading them. He drew near to Jesus to kiss him, but Jesus said to him, 'Judas, would you betray the son of man with a kiss?' And when those who were about him saw what would follow, they said, 'Lord, shall we strike with the sword?' And one of them struck the slave of the high priest and cut off his right ear. But Jesus said, 'No more of this!' And he touched his ear and healed him.
>
> Then Jesus said to the chief priests and captains of the temple and elders, who had come out against him, 'Have you come out as against a robber, with swords and clubs? When I was with you day after day in the temple, you did not lay hands on me. But this is your hour, and the power of darkness.' Then they seized him and led him away.

According to John (18.1-11)

The first three Gospels express in all kinds of ways their conviction that Jesus always spoke and acted on the basis of the most profound union with his Father. That aspect of Jesus' personality is stressed most strongly in the work of the Fourth Evangelist, John – in his passion narrative as well. In it he brings out even more explicitly than the others the extent to which Jesus dominates the drama. That in Gethsemane Jesus prayed to be spared from fearful suffering is a feature in the accounts in the other three Gospels which does not fit into John's picture of Jesus. At the end of the last supper Jesus indeed goes with his disciples to the garden, here called an orchard, but Judas immediately arrives with a great crowd. John has made it even larger, with a detachment of Roman soldiers. He speaks of a 'cohort', which would be a troop of 600 soldiers. Perhaps by this he means to indicate that the Roman authorities were already involved in the arrest. At all events, it is certain that he wants to magnify the contrast beween the power of Jesus' enemies and his defence-lessness in the usual sense of that word. Judas does not need to point him out, because Jesus introduces himself, and does so with such overwhelming majesty that the whole troop, including Judas, falls to the ground. The double meaning of the word with which Jesus makes himself known is very much in John's style. At first sight 'I am' means no more than 'I am the one you are looking for'. At the same time it points to the way in which in the Fourth Gospel Jesus indicates his origin from God, the God who had formerly revealed himself to Moses as 'I am'. There is also no mention of panic among the disciples and their flight: as the good shepherd, Jesus takes charge of them and himself sees that no one can be confused with them. In his prayer at the end of the last supper he had said that he would not let one of them be lost, and the evangelist points out that he immediately fulfils this divine saying. Finally, at the end of John's account we can see that he knows some of the traditions of the three other evangelists, elaborated with the proper names of the people involved.

When Jesus had spoken these words (the prayer to his Father at the supper), he went forth with his disciples across the Kidron valley, where there was an orchard which he and his disciples entered. Now Judas, who betrayed him, also knew the place; for Jesus often met there with his disciples. So Judas, procuring a band of soldiers and some officers from the chief priests and the Pharisees, went there with lanterns and torches and weapons. Then Jesus, knowing all that was to befall him, came forward and said to him, 'Whom do you seek?' They answered him, 'Jesus of Nazareth.' Jesus said to them, 'I am (the one).' Judas, who betrayed him, was standing with them. When he said to them 'I am (the one),' they drew back and fell to the ground. Again he asked them, 'Whom do you seek?' And they said, 'Jesus of Nazareth.' Jesus answered, 'I told you that I am he; so, if you seek me, let these men go.' This was to fulfil the word which he had spoken, 'Of those whom thou gavest me I lost not one.' Then Simon Peter, having a sword, drew it, and struck the high priest's slave and cut off his right ear. The slave's name was Malchus. Jesus said to Peter, 'Put your sword into its sheath; shall I not drink the cup which the Father has given me?'

Thus each of the four evangelists has put his own stamp on the facts about Jesus' passion, which he knew from oral traditions and traditions which had already been put down in writing. I now want to go on to illustrate this further from the words which Jesus spoke when he was hanging on the cross.

The seven words of Jesus from the cross

Lovers of classical music know the piece that Joseph Haydn wrote on 'The Seven Words of Jesus on the Cross'. He composed it at the request of a priest from the Spanish city of Cadiz. There, as in many other southern cities, it was the custom to have a kind of liturgy in Holy Week which took the following form. A priest read the first word, 'Father, forgive them, for they know not what they do.' He gave a short meditation on it, and then instrumental music was played which expressed the mood in sound. The same thing happened with each of the other six words: Jesus' promise to the 'penitent thief' came next; then his command to his mother and the beloved disciple; his exclamation 'I thirst'; his cry of abandonment expressed in the words of Psalm 22, his exclamation 'It is finished', and his last words: 'Into thy hands I commend my spirit.' Haydn composed the seven slow movements for a small orchestra, on each occasion following on from a bass voice which repeated the word from the cross. He composed an introduction to the whole work and added a conclusion which evoked the burial immediately after Jesus' death. He later wrote that it had not been simple to compose these seven slow movements, each of which had to last ten minutes. However, the work soon became famous, and with its help countless people have meditated on the last words of Jesus.

Do these words take on added depth when we remember that they were themselves the fruit of the meditations of the early Christians?

The only utterance of Jesus given by Mark is the prayer, 'My

101

God, my God, why have you forsaken me?', the cry with which Psalm 22 begins. According to Mark, Jesus prayed these words in his own language, Aramaic. The repeated 'My God', in that language, 'Eloi', sounded like the name of the prophet Elijah. People liked to appeal to this holy man as a helper in distress, above all to support pious people in the hour of their death. The bystanders did not want to know that Jesus was crying to his God and they said mockingly that he was calling on Elijah for help. One of them then set a sponge with a refreshing drink on a long reed and put it to Jesus' lips to make him live a bit longer, so that they could see if Elijah would still come to help him.

Whereas Matthew takes this over from Mark almost unchanged, Luke omits this prayer by Jesus and the mockery which follows. Perhaps it did not fit in with the picture which this sensitive and humane writer had formed of his saviour. At all events, as the last word of Jesus he chooses a line from another Psalm, prefaced with the intimate form of address to God, 'Father, into your hands I commend my spirit,' or in more modern language, 'I put my life in your hands and entrust it to your care.'

Before this saying Luke has two other sayings of Jesus, completely in the spirit of his Gospel, in which mercy and forgiveness are emphasized so strongly. When they crucified him, Luke writes, Jesus said, 'Father, forgive them, for they know not what they do', and rather later, when the man crucified to the right of him shows signs of penitence, the assurance to him, 'Truly I say to you, today you shall be with me in paradise.'

None of this – the total abandonment of Jesus, expressed in his cry of prayer, the bitter mockery of the bystanders and of the two others who were crucified with him, or the darkness over the land and the rending of the curtain of the temple – fits into the picture which John had formed. There is something regal about the scene in John, an element of royal repose. Friends stand round the cross: some women, among whom are his mother and the disciple whom he specially loved. Jesus addresses his last will and testament to them. To his mother, he says, 'Woman, behold your son,' and then to the disciple, 'Behold your mother'. Perhaps they both represent what Jesus leaves behind, or rather what he will bring to life by his 'loving to the uttermost': a community of people who care for one another and thus begin to put into practice what he had called his only commandment.

Then Jesus has to do something else that had been written in a prophetic psalm about him. He obediently drinks the vinegar which was given to him when he exclaimed, 'I thirst.' We should then read a note of triumph into the saying with which he ends his life, so utterly devoted to manifesting God's love to the world: 'It is accomplished!'

Who were responsible for Jesus' death?

After a few minutes of quiet reflection someone mentioned a recollection which had come back to her. In middle school she had had to translate passages from the Greek philosopher Plato. His book *The Republic* had impressed her a great deal at that time. In the form of conversations, it deals with all kinds of questions about the establishment of a just society. The passage that she remembered says that people must regard you as a righteous person if you are to be given a responsible post in their society. But what does that mean for someone who is all of a piece, who doesn't just want to *seem* to be righteous but actually wants to *be* just? The woman still recalled the answer to the question very well: 'Such a man will be scourged, tortured, his eyes will be put out and finally he will be crucified.' She had asked her teacher whether in this passage Plato had foretold the death of Christ four centuries later. All the class had laughed at her, and the teacher didn't give her a reply. Now she thought that Plato had written this on the basis of his insight into human nature: we cannot tolerate a fellow human being who is one hundred per cent good because he or she comes over to us as a living reproach; such a person begins to irritate us more and more, so that finally we resolve to do away with him or her. That could be the deepest reason for the execution of Jesus, the purest human being who ever lived, and who for that reason had aroused increasing hostility and even hatred among those of his people who seemed to be righteous.

Hence the question which had occurred to her: if the death of Jesus happened as a result of a resistance to good that is in all of us, can you then say that as a result we are all guilty of his death? Or is that too far-fetched?

There was no reply to this question. I then mentioned that in the time of Plato, a Jew on the other side of the Mediterranean was talking about the death of particularly good men. I was thinking of the great leader Ezra, and the prayer which has been preserved in chapter 9 of the biblical book of Nehemiah. It contains a confession of guilt. The disasters which had afflicted Jersualem and Judah, the exile in Babylon and the setbacks experienced by those who returned to Jerusalem were all punishments from God for the mistakes made by their forefathers. One of these was, 'They killed your prophets' (Neh.9.26). That had happened a long time beforehand, in the time of the kings. Nowhere was it said of these men that they were completely righteous. Certainly they themselves felt that they had been called by the God who was utterly righteous, who could not tolerate any injustice and oppression among his people. He sent them as prophets, his spokesmen, to complain about misdeeds and to threaten punishment. They did that, confronting kings and priests and the propertied classes. As a result they were arrested and killed, on the pretext that they were undermining society and endangering national security and prosperity.

After Ezra, the death of the prophets remained a fixed theme in the penitential prayers of the Jewish people. Jesus was not saying anything surprising when he once exclaimed over the city of Jerusalem, 'You kill the prophets and stone those who are sent to you.' However, he saw himself as the one who was bringing the sequence of prophets to an end, the last one sent by God to his people. He boldly went to Jerusalem to make known God's last call for conversion. However, it seemed impossible to the Jewish leaders that this man from Nazareth could be a prophet, a man sent from God. For God had bound himself to the Torah for ever, and in it had also ordained sacrificial worship for the temple.

Jesus proclaimed to ordinary people a 'kingdom of God' in which the Torah no longer had a role. He had criticized temple worship, in action as well as words. If there was a supernatural power behind him, as ordinary people believed, then this could only be God's opponent: Satan, Beelzebul.

Perhaps universal human antipathy to a person of complete integrity also played a part in the elimination of Jesus. But the most important conscious motive of the Jewish leaders was still, it seems to me, their concern to safeguard Jewish teaching and the Jewish way of life against the influence of a religious anarchist – which is what Jesus was in their eyes. They were convinced that they knew the will of God best and that their people had to live in accordance with this will. This conviction was deeply rooted in them, and at the same time it was inextricably bound up with their own interests. For them it was inconceivable that God should come up with a new initiative. Perhaps they had still expected such an initiative in the person of a royal Messiah from the dynasty of David, the glorious commander of a military force which would drive the Romans out of the land of the Jews. Something like that. But it was impossible that God should want to say and do something new through this poor carpenter from Nazareth with his alternative teaching and practices. Perhaps that is the charge that one could make against these anxious leaders: they had so encapsulated 'the living God' in their familiar patterns that he could not longer come up with anything new.

Here, by a different route, we came back to the question about who was responsible for Jesus' death. This gave me the opportunity to point to a tendency that we see at work right through the passion narratives: Pilate's share in this responsibility is diminished and that of the Jews is increased.

As to Pilate, from historical sources of this time he emerges as an ambitious and harsh, even pitiless man. After holding his post for ten years he was replaced because he had massacred Samaritans without sufficient reason. He was therefore accused before the Roman legate of Syria and then recalled to Rome. There is no mention in the Gospels of his bad points. He is an ordinary Roman official who condemns an innocent person to be crucified under pressure from the Jews and against his better judgment.

It seems probable that in this conception of things we have an expression of Christian concerns. Christians had spread all over the Roman world and wanted to be regarded as loyal citizens. People could not be given grounds for saying that the leader of the Christians, Jesus, had been condemned as a political troublemaker. It is certainly no coincidence that this is particularly stressed by Luke, who brings the Roman world of Caesar Augustus into his story right at the beginning of his Gospel, and whose plan is to write a second book about the expansion of the church throughout the empire.

In Mark we read that when Pilate asked Jesus, 'Are you the king of the Jews,' he replied, 'You say so.' While the Jews continue with their accusations, Pilate asks Jesus, 'Why do you give no reply?', but Jesus says no more. Pilate is amazed. At this point Luke adds that Pilate said to the Jewish leaders and to the people, 'I find no fault in this man.' Luke is the only evangelist who has Jesus next brought to the Galilean king Herod, who is in the city. There, too, Jesus is silent, and he also undergoes the mockery there in silence. After that Pilate says yet again, 'I have found no fault in this man, nor has Herod.' Finally, after the Barabbas scene, Pilate says once more, 'I have found nothing in him deserving of death.' Here Luke seems to want to say to his Roman readers, 'Don't be disturbed about us. Our leader was indeed crucified on the orders of a Roman, but this Roman himself asserted three times that Jesus was not guilty of rebellion in any way whatever.'

John makes Jesus hold two conversations with Pilate, in a dramatic scene of overwhelming power. He achieves this by having the Jews outside the court of judgment and Jesus inside. After the first conversation with Jesus, Pilate goes out to them and then says to the Jews: 'I find no fault whatsoever in him.' He still has Jesus scourged, then brings him outside and again says, 'Behold, I bring him out to show that I find no fault at all in him.' He repeats this yet again, and then finally yields to the Jews who are screaming, 'If you let this man go, you are no friend of Caesar.'

This tendency to exonerate Pilate established itself in the Christian tradition. In the apocryphal Gospel of Peter it is Herod, not Pilate, who pronounces the death sentence. According to the early church author Tertullian, Pilate was secretly a Christian. Later, in legends, he is even described as a martyr, and in one of the Christian churches he appears on the calendar of saints!

Parallel to the theme of having Pilate declare Jesus' innocence, which we might call a political motive, there is another one, that of fixing the responsibility for the execution of Jesus on the Jews. That is particularly clear in Matthew. I have just said that for him the new community of Christians is the new Israel, new,

106

because the old Israel in its entirety has rejected its Messiah. That motive emerges from small details in this passion narrative, where for example Matthew adds 'of the people' wherever the leaders occur; and where Mark writes that 'they' cried out for the death of Jesus, Matthew changes this to 'all'.

That emerges quite explicitly where Pilate is talking with the Jews about the possibility of letting Jesus go free instead of a certain Barabbas. Then it is Matthew who describes how Pilate received a message from his wife advising him, 'Have nothing to do with this just man, for I have suffered much over him today in a dream.' For the evangelist Matthew, the dream is a means by which God reveals his will. We have only to think of his stories about the birth of Jesus and the flight to Egypt.

When Pilate achieves nothing and finally has to yield to the pressure from the Jews, Matthew makes this Roman perform a typically Jewish gesture. In the law of Moses it was laid down that when anyone was murdered by an unknown person, the chief men in a city had to wash their hands and thus show that their hands had not shed his blood. 'I wash my hands' had also become a stereotyped expression which was sometimes used in the Psalms: 'I wash my hands in innocence.' That is what Matthew now makes Pilate do, and in so doing he says, 'I am innocent of this blood; you must take responsibility.' Thereupon 'the whole people' replies, 'His blood be on us and on our children.' That really means that they, the Jews, pronounce the death penalty on Jesus; his blood has to be shed and the Jews take responsibility for it, in the name of future generations as well.

I felt increasingly angry while I was talking about this outcry by the Jews. It has done such untold harm, or rather, it has served as a justification for so much evil that has been done to the Jews. I said what I would like: I would like all teachers of religion, and preachers, and interpreters of the Bible, always to say and to write at this point, 'Look, this is not historical. The Jews never shouted this out. It's part of Matthew's imagination.' Granted, it's a theological fantasy, understandable in the light of his view of the new community of Christians, composed of Jews and non-Jews. He saw them as the new Israel which had taken the place of the old: the old Israel had forfeited its privileges by rejecting Jesus as Messiah. It is Matthew who makes

Jesus say in chapter 23 of his Gospel, at the end of his parable about the wicked men in the vineyard, 'The kingdom of God shall be taken from you and given to a people which brings forth its fruits.' Matthew makes this view quite specific, in true Jewish fashion, in his passion narrative: the Jews have taken on responsibility for Jesus' death.

I would also want to stress the unhistorical elements in the Gospel stories about Judas. We have to realize that in other languages this word sounds even more like the word Jew than it does in Dutch or English. The Greek for Jew is *Ioudaios* and for Judas *Ioudas*, and it's the same in Latin. Judas is 'the Jew'. We can no longer discover with any certainty what motives drove Judas to his deed. It could be that he believed more strongly than the other eleven in his master, and that in his impatience he wanted to create a situation in which Jesus, always so restrained about himself, was forced openly to confess who he was, the Messiah.

It was the storytellers who began to attribute baser motives to Judas. We can see that, for example, at the beginning of the passion narrative. After a woman has anointed the head of Jesus with precious balsam during a meal in Bethany, Mark goes on to say, 'And Judas Iscariot, one of the twelve, went to the high priests to deliver him over to them. When they heard this they were overjoyed and promised to give him money, and he sought how he could find a good opportunity to hand him over to them.' So in Mark it is the leaders who raise the question of money. Matthew tells the story differently. He says that Judas went to the high priests and said to them, 'What will you give me if I hand him over to you?' According to Matthew it is Judas' greed which makes him perform this action.

In John we can see the same tendency. In the story of the woman who anointed Jesus, Mark and Matthew report that some of the disciples protested and said, 'This precious balsam should have been sold for a high price and the money given to the poor.' In John's version this becomes, 'But Judas, one of his disciples, who was to betray him, said, "Why was not this balsam sold for three hundred pieces of silver and the money given to the poor?" However, he said this not because he was concerned for the poor but because he was a thief and stole money from the purse which he looked after.'

This is the way in which the first narrators made all kinds of additions in connection with the motives which contributed to the execution of Jesus. However, this does not disguise the main point: Jesus became the victim of an interplay of religious and political authorities which had an interest in doing away with him. When we considered this in our discussion, someone pointed out that this historical fact brings the execution of Jesus closer to us, makes it more vivid. For we hear more and more often how in many countries people who stand up for their exploited and downtrodden fellow-citizens suffer the same fate as Jesus. They are treated as criminals, tortured and put to death by authorities who do not want to give up their privileges. So in this way the account of the execution of Jesus takes on a topicality which it did not have for our parents and grand-parents: they did not hear of such torture and execution every day.

The cross as a symbol of redemption

However, the cross was vivid to them in the deeper sense which has always had a central place in Christian conviction. Here the crucifixion of Jesus has to do with *everyone's* innermost being, *everyone's* attitude to God, and also with sin and guilt and liberation from them, with forgiveness and reconciliation. People have liked to see the shape of the cross as pointing to this deep and universal significance: the vertical beam indicates that God above and man below meet in the crucified Jesus: his outstretched arms on the horizontal beam represent the longing to involve all people in this encounter.

The crucifixion is inexhaustible, infinitely rich in meaning. It can be approached from all kinds of perspectives. When we began reflecting on them that evening someone asked a question which can serve as a starting point for one of these perspectives. I mean the question about the significance of the passage from Plato: if the real reason for killing Jesus stemmed from a resistance to the good that is in all of us, could you then say that we all bear responsibility for this death?

Before attempting an answer, I would like to make clearer precisely what is meant by this opposition to *the good* (as an impersonal ideal) in terms of opposition to *someone* (a person) who makes a demand on you. In the Jewish view this was not, as in Plato, the completely righteous man who makes an appeal to your conscience without knowing it, but God, the partner in the covenant, who through his prophets called on the rich and the powerful to treat everyone justly. You could describe their resistance to this as their anxiety about losing what they had earned. Where do you end up if you accept this demand of God to share everything out honestly?

In Jesus this call rang out far more clearly and more piercingly, as the call of a Father who loves all his children and wants them to accept this love and let it flow out to others. I shall put in my own words what he found necessary if we are to be open to it: 'If you hold on tightly to what you have earned, your possessions, your judgments on people, your system of ideas and rules of behaviour, so that you keep your fellow human beings at a safe distance and shut them out, then you are cutting yourselves off from God, you are excluding yourselves from this stream of love which is his nature.'

Our spontaneous human response to this challenge from Jesus is anxiety. What happens if we follow his call? If we share what we have, if we are open to everyone, don't put labels on people, forgive whatever other people do to us, where does that get us? Ordinary people who listened to Jesus perhaps thought: Yes, that's true, it must be like that. They felt the living power which came out of this preaching. Perhaps some religious leaders also sensed deep in their hearts that things really must be like this, that God wanted them to be in accordance with Jesus' experience of him. But if you act like this, where does it get you? What happens to your position, your reputation, your power, your money, what happens to the whole system with which all this is bound up, the sacred laws and customs? They had more to lose than ordinary people. Therefore he accepted that death. He counted on the truth of what he had said so succinctly, 'Anyone who loses his life will gain it.'

The question was whether we are all responsible for the death of Jesus. Many Christians over the course of centuries have said 'Yes' to it. I can recall from my schooldays the first line of an old Dutch poem, ''Twas not the Jews, Lord Jesus, who crucified Thee.' It doubtless continued with the penitent confession, 'We, I, did that.' Thus countless Christians feel personally involved in the suffering and death of Jesus: they themselves inflicted this suffering on him.

Those who cannot enter into such a 'mystical' experience, a bond which brings the event of the cross so close over the centuries, can perhaps also come to share in the responsibility in another way. We still do to our fellow human beings, time and again, what was done to Jesus then – not so radically and with such bloodshed, but also in ways which are very wounding and very painful for them. In quite subtle ways we can exclude, humiliate, write off other people, regard them as dead. The deepest reason why we crucify our fellow human beings in this way is our anxiety at losing what we have acquired and the defences that we have built up around ourselves. Ultimately it is our basic anxiety about death which prevents us human beings from arriving at the love to which Jesus invited us. He becomes the victim of our universal anxiety about death. In this sense we are involved with those who crucified him.

He voluntarily accepted this death, about which we are all so worried. In the light of Easter his disciples began to see that this was an act of 'love to the uttermost' and that here, in particular, God was utterly behind him. This meant that in his death God accepts us human beings, with this basic anxiety and with all the evil that we do to our fellow human beings as a result. Being accepted by God means forgiveness of all this, a clean sheet, a new beginning.

What we see among the first disciples is the consequence of that belief. It is as though they have left the past behind them and begun on a new life. They no longer betray anxiety at persecution, imprisonment and death. And above all, they form communities from which all earlier discrimination and enmity has disappeared; they accept one another as brothers and sisters. From then on the love which Jesus proclaimed and experienced is their only criterion.

I sometimes hear of people who have been told that they haven't long to live and how after they have come to accept the fact they begin to live much more intensively and with much more awareness. They arrive at unsuspected openness and depth in their relationship with husband, wife or friends. That makes me think that there is something in us human beings that makes us begin to live much more humanely when we give up our fight for the preservation of what seems to make up our lives.

It is often objected that our belief in God has grown out of a desire, a longing that we cannot fulfil. People say that evolution has ended up at the unfortunate creature called man. Man is an animal, an organic being which perishes. However, this animal has become so refined that it is aware of itself and of space and time outside the little world in which it lives. An animal which does not think dies without knowing that that is the end of it. Man, with his sense of the wide world around him, sees his death coming and resists this inevitable disintegration, this dissolution into the matter from which we came into being. So he creates for himself a divine world in which he will live on after his death. That is the origin of the phenomenon of religion. However, this theory does not match the known facts. Israelite and Jewish people believed in their God for centuries; they lived with him as a partner and sometimes passionately fought for this relationship at the risk of their lives, without any hope of a 'hereafter'. Only in the course of the second century before Christ did the expectation come alive among a particuar group of Jews that God would one day replace this evil world with a new one, in which people who had died would have a part. Only then did they begin to expect a 'resurrection of the dead' as one feature of this renewal at the end of time, historical time. The belief that after his death Jesus had been taken up into the life of God was certainly put into words in the framework of these Jewish expectations, in terms of resurrection from the dead, but it did not emerge from these hopes. Jesus' sense of God, his ministry and his acceptance of death were too unheard-of for that, not fitting in with any pattern of expectation.

Over against the view that belief in God emerged from the longings of that frustrated being called man, we talk in terms of 'revelation'. The Creator made himself known to Israel as being 'personal'. He brought these encounters to a climax, that is to the point of the deepest possible intimacy, in Jesus, in whom he shared our life, up to and including death. In this way he seeks to free us from our anxiety and so liberate us for the love which makes us akin to him. All this is summed up in the cross, and that is why it is such an inexhaustible symbol for us.

9 Born of the Virgin Mary: Do I Have to Believe That?

Towards the end of a long conversation about belief and unbelief one of those involved came up with the question of the virginity of Mary: that she became the mother of Jesus without having had anything to do with a man. The question was, 'If you want to be a Christian, do you have to believe that miracle?' I replied that I could not go into the question so late in the evening, that it was far too complicated. But I promised the group that I would try to put down on paper what I thought might be a satisfactory answer. I shall try to do that here. It's going to be a long explanation. For first of all we have to see precisely where the virgin birth comes in the Bible, what is said and how it came to be written. After that comes the question of what you might mean if you said that you believed in the virgin birth.

First of all the facts. In the New Testament the miraculous birth, or rather conception, is related by two authors, Matthew and Luke. Each describes it in the first chapter of his Gospel. In Luke, the angel Gabriel first announces to the old priest Zechariah in the temple at Jerusalem that he will have a son by an equally old woman, and that he is to call this son John. Five months later the same Gabriel again goes off to announce the birth of a son, this time in the north of the land, in Nazareth, to a Mary who is betrothed to a certain Joseph, a distant descendant of David. When Mary asks how it can be possible to have a son without sexual intercourse with a man, the angel replies that this miracle will take place in her through the creative power of God, the 'Holy Spirit'. Later on in Luke's story the two promised children come into the world, born in the usual way, the same as any other children.

The account in Matthew is a bit different. For him, Joseph and Mary live in Bethlehem, not in Nazareth. That is where they have their home. One day Joseph notices that his bride-to-be is pregnant. Then an angel of God appears to him in a dream and reassures him by declaring that the child in her womb is 'of the Holy Spirit'. When, a little later, Matthew begins to describe the arrival of wise men from the East in Jerusalem, the indication of time he gives is 'when Jesus was born in Bethlehem'. That is the only statement he makes about the birth of Jesus.

Thus we see that the miracle of a conception without the involvement of a man is mentioned in these two stories only when the birth of Jesus is announced by an angel. Neither Matthew nor Luke goes further into this miraculous origin of Jesus in his story about him.

The two other evangelists, Mark and John, usually speak of Jesus as the son of Joseph, as if they had never heard of this miraculous conception. Paul mentions the birth of Jesus once, in his letter to the Galatians. Before the coming of Christ we were not free, he said, we were slaves, 'but when the fullness of time had come, God sent his only son, born of a woman, born under the law, to turn us slaves into free men, to make us sons...' Among the Jews, 'born of a woman' was the usual way of denoting an ordinary person. From this it is quite clear that what we have come to call the miracle of Jesus' birth from a virgin hardly seems to have concerned the first generation of Christians at all, if indeed they even knew anything about it. Matthew and Luke describe it, but they evidently did not find it important enough to refer to again in their accounts of Jesus' life and fate.

In that case, why did they relate it, and above all, where did they get their information from? They wrote their Gospels towards the end of the 80s. How did Luke know at that stage, more than three-quarters of a century later, that an angel named Gabriel had spoken like this to Mary one day in Nazareth, and how did Matthew know of this angel who had informed Joseph in a dream in Bethlehem?

If we are going to give any kind of satisfactory answer to these questions, we must try to immerse ourselves in the ways in which these early Christians thought and spoke; in other words, we must let our imaginations work. And we have to do that at three points, or better, in three areas. The first I would call the sense of newness among the earliest generations of Christians. By that I mean the conviction and the experience that the God of Israel had begun something completely new in the person of Jesus, something that had ushered in a new and definitive period of time – in terms of Jewish expectations, the last days or the end time.

Then we shall try to become more familiar with another area, with the ways in which people of this time and culture used to describe the beginnings of the lives of their exceptionally great men.

Finally, we shall look at a third area, less extensive, but certainly important for our subject: the differences between the evangelists Matthew and Luke in their ways of thinking and writing. For that must be the reason why their stories about the beginning of Jesus' life seem to be so different.

The creative Spirit of God in action

I took the expression 'sense of newness' which I've just used from the title of a book that I once saw as a first-year theologian and probably never read. It was about the New Testament. I certainly remember the title well. It was in German: *Christentum als Neuheitserlebnis* (Christianity as an Experience of Newness). That is in fact the basic experience which runs right through the New Testament. God had set something new in motion. He had begun this with the appearance of Jesus of Nazareth. Jesus proclaimed, in the footsteps of John the Baptist, that God would come soon to usher in his rule, his kingdom. The way in which Jesus did this was very surprising. It seemed as though he himself was already at home in that kingdom of his 'Father', as he called God. He had inside knowledge of the great desire of that Father, the desire to bring all his people together into one family, a divine family, in which they would all come completely into their own. He used his exceptional gifts to heal people and to free them from the demons who tormented them, in order to make them see all this, how people could become whole. His short life was one great invitation to the Jews to prepare them-

115

selves for the final consummation, which was imminent. Here Jesus paid no attention to the sacred regulations, the rules of living which concerned the sabbath and purity and temple worship. These now belonged definitively to the past, and that was finished with. In doing this he aroused increasingly strong resistance among the Jewish leaders who had to implement the age-old regulations. That was their duty, so they could not do other than banish from society this newcomer from Galilee, who turned people's heads and taught them to be disobedient to the laws of God.

What happened after that was quite unheard of: God made clear to Jesus' companions after his death, by the appearances, that he had raised up the dead Jesus to himself, to his life beyond our imagining. That, too, was new and completely unexpected. Jesus was quickly referred to, in an amazingly daring phrase, as the 'firstborn from the dead', as if the world of the dead had suddenly become fertile and had given birth to new man, a first child who would be followed by countless many more.

It meant that the fatal doom which hung over all mankind had now been lifted. Indeed there was a new creation, and Christians could even experience it in their own lives. They felt that they were new men and women, with a new perspective, freed from their past and from all the anxiety, frustration and sinfulness which had been characteristic of it. Above all they learned to treat their fellow human beings in a completely new way. The same thing was true of the adults who joined a Christian community elsewhere in the empire. For each of them this was a break with the past and the beginning of a new life, a kind of resurrection from the dead, a sharing in the new life of Christ.

The first disciples were all Jews, and in the light of their tradition, their thought-world, only one fact in the Bible was comparable with what God was now doing: the first creation of his world. True, sometimes he had blown in history with his creative breath or wind – for that is the meaning of the word which is always translated 'Spirit' – over people who had a special task, as leaders or prophets, concerned with the welfare of God's people. Then this spirit blew on them or came upon them and they became different people, capable of doing more than they had ever dreamed of. Now, however, the spirit of God seized all Christians and inspired them, made them enthusiastic witnesses, which was what the prophet Joel had once said would happen in the end time, the last days. Then the spirit would come upon old and young, man and woman, slave and free. That was what was happening now.

I also mentioned in passing another experience of Christians in the first half of the century: most of their fellow-Jews could not see this new development as a work of the spirit of God. On the contrary, for them Jesus of Nazareth was and remained a man who had departed from the practice of the Jewish faith at essential points and had involved other Jews in his apostasy. He had been rightly condemned by the Supreme Council and handed over to the Romans. In the eyes of true believing Jews, for followers of this man now to praise him as the longed-for anointed of God, the Messiah, was blasphemous nonsense. The fact that during those years an increasing number of non-Jews, uncircumcised and unclean pagans, joined them, proved even more how far they had departed from the faith of the fathers.

Even at Jesus' baptism in the Jordan...

As I have already said, in hindsight the disciples of Jesus could already see the renewing work of God's spirit in his unprecedented ministry. That had begun when he had gone to the Jordan and there received baptism from John. Towards the year 70 Mark wrote his Gospel, probably the first work in that genre. He began his account with a short sketch of John's preaching, leading into the story of the baptism of Jesus. We can get a good deal out of these few lines. This is what they say.

> In those days Jesus came from Nazareth in Galilee and was baptized by John in the Jordan. And when he came up out of the water, immediately he saw the heavens opened and the Spirit descending upon him like a dove; and a voice came from heaven, 'Thou art my beloved Son; with thee I am well pleased.'

I often say that three elements can usually be pointed out in any passage from the Gospels: a historical reminiscence, traces of the activity of the Christians who handed down this remi-

117

niscence by word of mouth, and finally something of the style and concern of the author.

The historical reminiscence here is the fact that Jesus had himself baptized. That is certainly historical. Christians would never have made it up. After Easter they began to recognize Jesus as the Son of God, and it is inconceivable that they would have made him undergo a 'baptism of repentance for the forgiveness of sins'. For some of them the fact that Jesus was baptized even became a problem, as we shall soon see.

Then there is the vision of Jesus, who saw the spirit descending on him, and the voice from heaven, speaking to him in words from the Old Testament. It is clear that here we have an expression of the belief of Christians. After Easter and Pentecost they tried to put into words the incredible new thing that God had done and was doing, in Jesus and in themselves, using familiar terms and imagery to help them. The spirit of God had come upon Jesus incomparably more strongly than upon any great man from the biblical past. And what God had said to a king of David's house in Psalm 2, 'You are my son', and to his devoted servant in Isaiah 42, about his 'good pleasure' in him, had become more than true in Jesus.

Finally, the author Mark found this a good beginning for his story. In this way he presented the main figure directly to his readers. It would then strike them that only the demons realized something of Jesus' supernatural power: he was their master, and he drove them out of their victims. But the close disciples did not understand anything about him, still less did the Jewish leaders. Only when Jesus had followed the path of his suffering to the end did a Roman officer recognize his true nature: 'Truly this was the Son of God.' For that death in obedience to his Father for the good of mankind was an integral part of his person as a revealer of God's love.

It seems to me worth going on to see what the Evangelist Matthew does with the story of Mark I've just quoted. He was writing fifteen to twenty years later than Mark. In his community there were obviously people who had difficulty with the baptism of Jesus in the Jordan. Instead of saying to them, 'Just accept it, because that was clearly how God arranged things,' in true biblical fashion he incorporated this answer into his version of Mark's account. (The expression 'fulfil all righteousness' is Mat-

118

thew's way of saying 'do what God has ordained'.) See too how the heavenly voice here does not speak to Jesus, but about him.

> Then Jesus came from Galilee to the Jordan, to be baptized by John. John would have prevented him, saying, 'I need to be baptized by you, and do you come to me?' But Jesus answered him, 'Let it be so now; for thus it is fitting for us to fulfil all righteousness.' Then he consented. And when Jesus was baptized, he went up immediately from the water, and behold, the heavens were opened, and he saw the Spirit of God descending like a dove, and alighting on him; and lo, a voice from heaven, saying, 'This is my beloved Son, with whom I am well pleased.'

How the lives of famous men began

A man has to have had extraordinarily great influence and really to have seized the imagination of his contemporaries if he is to become a legend after his death. That still happened in the Middle Ages, for example with saints like Francis. It also happened in the cultural world in which the biblical narrators lived. Certain figures had played an unmistakable part in God's history with his people. Or to put it more precisely, people felt that God had seen that these great men were around at the critical moment. They were fond of expressing this in stories about the beginnings of the lives of such men, for example by describing how they were born when this was impossible from a human point of view: their parents were too old or their mother was barren. Another way of describing this was by saying that they escaped a deadly danger shortly after their birth by the miraculous disposition of God.

One example of the latter story is the tale of the baby Moses. Pharaoh had commanded that all the newborn Hebrew boy children were to be killed. Moses' mother then put him in a basket made of rushes which she had made watertight with asphalt and pitch, and left him in the reeds beside the Nile. In this way Moses escaped the massacre of the children. At that time a similar legend was going the rounds throughout the East about the first Semitic ruler of the world, King Sargon, who lived around 2300 BC. He, too, was put by his mother in such a

119

basket to become a foundling. Asphalt and pitch were quite common in Mesopotamia, whereas the material had to be imported into Egypt. For that reason it is also assumed that this old legend about Sargon was the model for the biblical narrator.

Those who believe in the Bible may perhaps object to assertions like this. Is this not a sign of lack of respect for the Bible, to put it no more strongly than that? In reply, I would want to say that this approach is just as much a sign of respect for the biblical narrators. It is a respect that requires us to try to imagine life in their world, their way of thinking and depicting things. Whenever we really want to listen to someone else, we are called on to put aside our own ideas of what must and what must not be the case and make ourselves completely open to these others. So it seems to me disrespectful to require the narrators from this biblical period to adapt themselves to Western European norms by which 'the truth' of their story is to be measured. Because of this I was glad to see the footnote which the Willibrordbijbel, the translation made by the Dutch Catholic Biblical Foundation, adds to the story in Exodus 2: 'The story of Moses' childhood is a real folk tale which has arisen out of the need to make the unknown youth of famous men correspond with their later greatness. This story shows great similarities with one about King Sargon of Akkad. The story seeks to show that God was already at work among his oppressed people without anyone suspecting the fact.'

I move on from the author of Exodus to a contemporary of Matthew and Luke, the great Jewish historian Flavius Josephus. In the year 93 or 94 he published his great work *Jewish Antiquities*. In it he presented to the educated reading public in the Roman empire a complete history of the Jewish people from the first beginnings to the year 66. He tells more about Moses than he found in the Bible. For even after the extent of the Bible had been fixed legends continued to form about this greatest figure from the Jewish past. Joseph draws on them in the same way as he draws on the Bible. So he describes how Amram, the father of Moses, saw God coming to him in a vision before Moses' birth. God announced to him that he would have a son who would rescue the people of the Hebrews from Egypt.

It would therefore be surprising if no legends about the beginning of Jesus' life were told among the Christians of this first

120

century, and if the evangelists Luke and Matthew did not borrow material from this for their accounts. Each did that in his own way. In their accounts of Jesus' public life and his passion they felt bound to the plan and material of their predecessor Mark and to other traditions which had become authoritative. But when it came to describing Jesus' origin, they could give their imagination freer rein. I shall now go into their stories in rather more detail. Only then can we speak meaningfully about the question of what we are to believe.

Luke's account

All we know of the evangelist whom we call Luke is what we can get out of his two-volume work dedicated to a certain Theophilus: the Gospel and the Acts of the Apostles. From that it emerges that he was probably not a Jew by birth and that he had had a very good training as a writer. He may well have been a 'godfearer', i.e. a sympathizer with the Jewish religion, and perhaps even a 'proselyte', someone who had associated himself with the Jewish people as closely as possible. At all events he had made himself thoroughly familiar with the Greek translation of the Old Testament, the Jewish Bible. In particular, he adopted the style of the old accounts and deliberately gave some parts of his work an authentically biblical character. That is particularly true of the accounts of the beginning of Jesus' life. He also uses this biblical style in the first sections of the book of Acts. In the later part, when Paul becomes increasingly involved in the Gentile world, and especially when he makes his last journey to Rome as a prisoner, Luke's style begins to resemble that of the secular historians.

Even someone who does not know Greek can get an idea of Luke's own style by putting his Gospel beside that of Mark. If you do that you can even see how he rewrites stories by Mark, clarifies details in them, and sometimes also leaves out things that do not fit in with his own picture of Jesus.

This man who made the Jewish Bible so much his own preserved his openness to the Gentile world. It is also striking that he assigns a greater role to women than his Jewish fellow-evangelists.

Luke has combined his account of the beginning of Jesus' life with a story about the birth of John the Baptist, and has done so in a very careful and artistic way. This will be even clearer to us if we recall one particular historical development, or rather historical chain of events. John the Baptist was already a much-discussed figure when Jesus was still living his life unknown in Nazareth. He had formed a group of dedicated disciples, and this group continued in existence after the Baptist had been arrested and killed. It seems that they continued to revere him as the last prophet, the revealer of God, the expected Messiah. Many of this group continued to confess him in this way when a similar group had formed round the crucified Jesus of Nazareth. You could call them two rival movements. They were still rivals towards the end of the first century. We can see this from the Fourth Gospel, which was written at that time.

In the marvellous hymn with which it begins, about the word which was with God and the light which shines in darkness, we suddenly have a passage about the man sent from God named John: 'He was not the light, but came to bear witness to that light.' A little further on there is another such interruption. The Baptist has declared that the one who comes after him is greater than he is. When the Gospel narrative proper begins, the Baptist says with great assurance, 'I am not the Messiah.' After that he directs his own disciples to Jesus, 'Behold the Lamb of God,' clearly in the hope that they will follow him. For, as he declares later on in the story, 'He must increase and I must diminish.'

The evangelist Luke chose a different way of clearly bringing out the role of the Baptist as a forerunner of Jesus. Along with all Christians, he regarded John as a prophet sent by God, above all because Jesus had spoken to this effect about John; indeed he had even said that John was the greatest of all those born of women. To do so, Luke used a narrative pattern with which he had become familiar from the Jewish Bible: someone who had fulfilled an important role in the life of God's people, and therefore had been sent by the God of Israel, was already announced to his parents before his birth. They were afraid of the heavenly visitant who came to say this to them; after assuring them that they had nothing to fear, this divine messenger announced what the promised child would be called and how he would later carry out the programme indicated by his name; if they asked a question, they were given an explanation and sometimes also a sign.

Luke has the birth of the Baptist, and then of Jesus, announced in accordance with this pattern. In this way he makes it possible for him to portray the future function of both figures: John the forerunner and Jesus the Messiah and Son of God. He does this in a marvellous mixture of parallels and contrasts. The Baptist is still part of the old order of things. The announcement of his birth happens where you would expect it, in the temple, to a man, an old priest, who cannot believe that his wife can still bear a child and who therefore is punished with dumbness. With Jesus, something completely new is beginning. The angel of God makes his proclamation not in the capital, the centre of Jewish worship, but in Galilee of the Gentiles, in the unknown place Nazareth, and does so not to an old man who is a priest but to a young woman, Mary, who is a virgin and who accepts this message. As a sign, she is told that her old kinswoman Elisabeth is in her sixth month of pregnancy.

The next part of Luke's story is quite sublime: Mary bravely undertakes the long journey to Elizabeth, who lives in Judaea, close to Jerusalem. When the two pregnant women meet, the unborn John already fulfils the function for which he is ordained: he greets the mother of the one whose forerunner he is to be!

After this, Luke first describes the birth of John, and then eight days later his circumcision and the giving of his name. Parallel to that he describes the same events in the case of Jesus, but in more detail: his birth, his circumcision and his naming. But after that he goes further. He knows that among the Jews something else happened on the fortieth day after the birth, i.e. the mother's purification, and he connects another custom with it, the dedication of the firstborn to God. Luke did not know the precise difference beween these two customs; the important thing for him is that the child Jesus is brought from Bethlehem to the temple in Jerusalem. In this way he can make his story end where it had begun. And again he brings together two old people, Simeon and Anna. After that Mary and Joseph return to Nazareth with their child Jesus.

When I have the chance to read this story in a group at Christmas, I do so first without the songs of praise, because I feel that these tend to destroy the structure. I'm referring, of course, to the long hymns of praise by Zechariah and Mary, and the shorter ones by the angelic host and by Simeon. Perhaps Luke inserted these very biblical compositions later.

Before we begin the reading I point out some details. First of all the census under the emperor Augustus. Luke uses this theme to make Joseph and Mary travel to Bethlehem, which he is the only biblical writer to call the city of David. For him and his readers the emperor Augustus was far more than a name. This ruler had died in the year 14, but he still lived on long in memories as the great peacemaker, the redeemer or saviour of the Roman empire. In some cities his birthday, 23 September, was celebrated as New Year's Day. The most powerful man in the world at that time had furthered the divine plan to have the ultimate peacemaker, the saviour of all men, born in Bethlehem. This is just a glance towards the wider world of men in which Jesus would later be proclaimed as saviour. Then the story again goes further into the milieu of pious Judaism. The men and women who appear in it all live blameless lives, in accordance with God's law. Luke evidently wants to emphasize that. His plan is to describe in the second half of his work, the Acts of the Apostles, how faith in Jesus the Messiah took root among the nations, the 'Gentiles', whereas most Jews could not take a step towards Jesus. He has this painful development announced by old Simeon in the final scene, in which Jesus is offered to God. The old man says to the mother of Jesus that 'this child is determined for the fall and rising of many in Israel, as a sign that shall be spoken against.' Even Mary herself will experience this division, as a 'sword through her soul' . Perhaps Luke is thinking here of what he is going to describe later, in chapter 11. A woman who was listening to Jesus cried out in excitement that it must be marvellous for his mother to have such a son. Jesus reacted by saying, 'Blessed are those who hear the word of God and do it.' Luke felt that this must have been hard on Mary and comforting for believers who came from the Gentile world. The important thing was belief, not kinship with Jesus, be it never so intimate. The readers of Luke's two-volume work had to learn awareness of this: they are not of Jewish origin, but by faith belong to the people of the Jewish Messiah.

Finally I tell people how Luke found the name of the angel who announces the births in the book of Daniel, the only place where Gabriel occurs. In Daniel 9, Gabriel declares to Daniel the course of history, at the end of which 'an anointed' will be killed.

The way in which Luke's apparently simple story is 'loaded' can thus be seen from the fact that he has woven together all kinds of things from the Old Testament – names, narrative forms and so on – with features which in fact depict the experiences of Christians.

The story of Matthew, the theologian

The story of the birth of Jesus in the Gospel of Matthew is no less complex, but in a very different way. It emerges from the whole of this Gospel that the author is a Jew and that he knows the Jewish Bible like a scribe. The Greek-speaking Christian community for which he writes consists predominantly of Jews, but at the same time it is open to new members from the world of non-Jews. In the 80s its break with 'official' Judaism had become complete. It looked upon itself as the true Israel which had recognized the promised Messiah, the Son of the living God, in the Jew Jesus, Son of David, and was ready to be guided by him and his commandments.

Matthew begins with the genealogy of Jesus, which indicates that Abraham was his father and so he was an authentic Jew, who moreover was descended from the house of David. In the last centuries before Christ, the construction of genealogies had become one way of demonstrating historical connections. If you open I Chronicles, you can see for yourself how a Jewish historian writing towards the year 300 BC summarizes the history of centuries. There is evidence that in the time of Jesus certain families preserved genealogies to prove their royal descent. A historian from the third century tells how Herod the Great had such papers belonging to well-known Jewish families burnt. That is understandable for a 'king of the Jews' whose father was an Idumaean, i.e. a descendant of the hated Edomites. At all events, Matthew so arranges the list as to arrive at three times fourteen generations between Abraham and Jesus, another customary way of expressing the belief that God had a hand in the history which led to the birth of the Messiah.

The long list of names is no dry summary to those who know the Old Testament well. The whole genealogy used to be sung in our monastery on Christmas Eve with a long series of notes on each name. With each name a whole series of stories passed through our minds, a great many elements from that century-long preparation which led up to the event.

It is striking that Matthew mentions the names of four women among all these men who father sons. They are not the famous mothers of the tribes of Israel, like Sarah, Rebecca and Rachel, but women who brought a forefather of Jesus into the world in an unusual way. First comes Tamar. In Genesis 38 we can read how she conceived her long-desired son by her father-in-law Judah: she dressed up as a prostitute and offered him her services. Then there is Rahab, the harlot of Jericho, no less quick-witted and energetic, according to the account in Joshua 2. Matthew regards her as the mother of Boaz, who becomes the great-grandfather of King David through his association with the Moabite woman Ruth. You can read about the remarkable way in which this association came about in the touching story in the Bible to which Ruth has given her name. Finally, David fathered his son Solomon by 'the wife of Uriah', a phrase with which Matthew recalls the uniquely powerful story in II Samuel 13: David possesses Bathsheba, the attractive wife of Uriah, and has her husband Uriah the Hittite murdered. You can read in the first chapters of the book of Kings how it was thanks to Bathsheba's support that Solomon became king after David.

It will have been clearer to the first readers of Matthew than it is to us why he chose precisely these four women. Legends had also come into being about them, precisely because they had played such a striking role in the history of God with his people. However, we know little of these stories. Perhaps Matthew thought of the way in which they had conceived their children against the customary rules, thus as it were pointing forward to the quite unusual way in which the Messiah was conceived. Another factor may have been that they were not Israelites by birth, and were therefore Gentiles; that was clear in the case of Ruth and Rahab, and presupposed in the case of Tamar and Bathsheba, the wife of Uriah the Hittite. In this way they already represented Matthew's concern, the incorporation of Gentiles into the new Israel.

The genealogy ends: '... Jacob was the father of Joseph, the husband of Mary, who gave birth to Jesus who was called the

Christ.' After the comment on the three times fourteen generations there follows the story about the problem which Joseph had when he saw that his fiancée was pregnant. On the instructions of the angel who appeared to him in a dream, he then made Mary officially his wife and in this way became the legal father of Jesus, who thus became 'son of David'.

It is worth remembering that Joseph is never mentioned in the recollections of the public ministry of Jesus. So it is understandable that when people told stories about the beginning of Jesus' life they looked for information in the stories in the book of Genesis about his great namesake, who was also the son of a Jacob. This Joseph played a major role in the migration of the family of Israel to Egypt. The most striking thing about this man was that he had significant dreams, which gained him the nickname 'the dreamer'. Clearly Matthew filled in Joseph's role along the lines of that model. This happens not only in the first story, in which an angel appears to him 'in a dream', but also in its sequel, in which he takes the child and his mother to Egypt and from there to the security of Nazareth, in each case on the basis of instructions which he receives in a dream.

However, Matthew first tells the story of the wise men from the East who came to Jerusalem to pay homage to the new-born king of the Jews: they had seen the rise of his star. It is worth our while remembering that something of this kind did not sound so strange in the world of the time as it does to us. Great importance was attached to unexpected phenomena in the heavens. These often announced the birth – or the death – of a great ruler. According to Cicero, the 'sages' in Persia, the astrologers, explained a strange light as a sign that someone had been born who would be a great danger to Asia: that was Alexander the Great. The emperor Nero (54-68) was very alarmed when a comet appeared several nights in succession. This was seen as a sign that an important man would die. He then had a number of men in high positions executed to make sure. Although 'magoi' (the word which Matthew uses here) are reported in the great cities, i.e. astrologers, soothsayers and magicians of all kinds, the home of the real astrologers was Babylonia, or, more generally, 'the East'. Balaam, the heathen seer in the story which appears in Numbers 22-24, also came from there. This man was commanded by the king of Moab to pronounce a curse on the disturbing people of Israel who had come out of Egypt. However, when he was in ecstasy, Balaam could pronounce nothing but blessings. His last visions are of the future ruler of Israel whom he describes like this: 'I see him, but not now; I behold him, but not nigh; a star shall come forth out of Jacob, and a sceptre shall rise out of Israel.' Did Matthew's wise men see this star arising?

In the reaction of King Herod and the Jewish leaders Matthew depicts something of what he and his community experienced to their sorrow. The mass of the Jewish people, who possessed the scriptures and knew of the Messiah from them, did not recognize him, whereas complete strangers, Gentiles, began to pay homage to him as the king of the nations. Matthew found the gifts that were offered to Jesus in Isaiah 60, where they are brought by the nations when the light of God has risen over Zion.

Herod's resolve to kill all the boys of two years old and under in Bethlehem and the countryside around fits in well with the character of this ruler. The Jewish historian Flavius Josephus described in detail how this king became increasingly suspicious and cruel. Shortly before his death, for example, he had three of his own sons killed. However, in his extensive account Josephus says nothing about the massacre of the infants in Bethlehem. Matthew introduces it into his story to indicate how, as the new Moses, Jesus takes over the functions of the first Moses and fulfils them: he too escapes from a massacre of children. In the same way, as the true son of God Jesus underwent the sojourn in Egypt experienced by Israel, the son. After their wanderings, Joseph brings the child and his mother safely to Nazareth, and there too, according to Matthew, a prophecy is fulfilled, although he does not indicate the prophetic book in which it can be found.

In the case of the grief of the mothers in Bethlehem, Matthew explicitly refers to the book of Jeremiah. In the word of God which appears in 31.16ff., Rachel laments over the loss of her children. She was the 'mother' of the tribes to the north of Jerusalem who had been deported by the Assyrians. Her tomb was located near to the village of Ramah. As a result of a misunderstanding long before the time of Matthew, this tomb was thought to be near Bethlehem. That is why the poetic saying could be used in connection with the massacre of the children. In the book of Jeremiah it is immediately followed by the promise that the children whom Rachel mourns will again return from the land of the enemy. However, at this time people felt no hesitation about applying a biblical saying detached from its immediate context.

Those are some comments on Matthew's story about the beginning of Jesus' life. I hope that they are enough to make it clear how much this story is loaded with the biblical knowledge which he and his community had acquired, and with insights into the person and life of Jesus, as the figure in whom so many of God's earlier dealings with his people had been fulfilled. For Matthew and his community he is the Messiah of Israel, and also the saviour of the nations: this had begun to be increasingly evident at this time, when Gentiles everywhere were flocking to the community centred on this saviour.

I should add here that the legends which Matthew narrates were not as strange to the people of that time as they are to us. The biographers of the Emperor Nero report that in the year 66, i.e. about twenty years before Matthew wrote his work, a king from distant Armenia came to Rome with a large entourage, to pay homage to the Emperor Nero. Princes from the great people of the Parthians were among his following. We are also told how this king of Armenia returned to his homeland 'by another way' from the one he had taken on his coming. One historian speaks of the king and his followers as *magoi*, wise men. Jewish readers of Matthew would not be surprised, either, at the news that Joseph had had to flee to Egypt. When king Solomon wanted to arrest the rebel Jeroboam, Jeroboam fled to Egypt. According to the book of Jeremiah, the prophet Uriah did the same thing after preaching against Jerusalem and the temple, thus attracting the king's attention. Some centuries later, the high priest followed this example to escape the policies of king Antiochus. So Joseph, too, fled to Egypt with the child Jesus. In commenting that this was the fulfilment of a saying of the prophet Hosea, 'Out of Egypt I called my son', Matthew confesses that while Israel was meant in that text, true sonship has only become a reality in Jesus.

I have used the word 'legends', and I'm not going to take it back. The infancy narratives of Luke and Matthew are certainly too well constructed, too well thought out to be called just legends, but at all events they do contain legendary elements. When Jesus made his first public appearance, no one was as yet interested in the circumstances of his birth. He had to die before he became the centre of the new and rapidly growing Christian movement. I referred above all to the enthusiastic woman who praised the mother of Jesus when she heard him and saw him at work. She cried out, 'Blessed is the womb that bore you and the breasts which you sucked!' But that was far from being a story about his birth. Probably stories of this kind were first told among Jewish Christians in Palestine. It was as it were in their blood to tell stories about facts from the past in which the hand of God was so clearly visible to them. Numerous stories in the old Bible bear witness to this. By being included in this book God's concern was recorded, in a sense given tangible form, at a particular moment. What I tried to say is this: in some cases the written form of a story represents only one moment in the flow of story-telling, which then becomes coagulated in that form. But the story-telling about the same fact developed further after that moment. I gave an example in connection with Moses, mentioning the account of how the birth of the liberator of the people was announced to his father Amram, which was not yet in existence when the text of the book of Exodus was fixed. The stories in Luke and Matthew doubtless take up tales which were going the rounds at that time among Christians. However, in their final form they are above all the result of the personal insights and the artistic skill of the two evangelists. Still, even there, yet more stories about the birth of Jesus were going the rounds, in increasing numbers, because the imagination of Jewish Christians continued to be active. There are more indications of this in some of the 'apocryphal' gospels. These not only give a great many more names, like Joachim and Anna for Mary's parents, but also relate all kinds of miracles which the child Jesus is said to have done. Once on a sabbath he modelled little birds out of clay. When someone commented on this violation of the sacred day of rest, Jesus clapped his hands and the birds flew away. He turned a friend who crossed him into a withered tree and cursed another, whereupon the youth immediately fell dead. This is the kind of way in which people fantasized about the divine child as a miracle worker in the making.

In comparison with the apocryphal writings, the sobriety and depth of Matthew and Luke stand out strongly. With a fine sensitivity to the nature of their stories, Matthew and Luke make the witnesses to the first days of Jesus' life vanish from the scene before his public ministry begins: the shepherds go back to their flocks and the wise men to their country. Only Luke tells another story about Jesus when he was twelve years old. He went with his parents to Jerusalem to worship. They missed him on the way back and eventually found him in the temple, where he was talking to the teachers. All the stress is laid on what Jesus then said to his mother, the first of his sayings which Luke reports to us, 'Did you not know that I had to be about my Father's business?' This expresses precisely what was to be a characteristic of the grown-up Jesus: his sense of being associated with God in a unique way, as Son.

We can now go into the question which was raised at the beginning, and which we can now put in this way: *must* we believe that Mary conceived her child through the working of God's creative spirit, without the involvement of any man?

Let me first point out that 'believe' and 'must' cannot go together. Believing, in the biblical sense, has to do with a relationship to a person, trust in and surrender to someone, to God. In such a relationship there can be no question of obligation or compulsion, something laid on us from outside.

Secondly, in this meaning of belief, we are not dealing with a fact, an event in itself, but with the significance given to it by the relationship. Here is an illustration from the Old Testament. On a certain day Jeremiah announced the coming destruction of the temple, because those who visited it were committing crimes against their fellow men. For some people Jeremiah was therefore a true spokesman of Yahweh, a prophet of Israel's God as they experienced him. Others regarded and treated Jeremiah as a blasphemer, because God himself had intended his temple to be his dwelling place for always. So these are different interpretations of the same event, deriving from different views of God.

131

The public ministry of Jesus, from his baptism in the Jordan to his death on the cross, was seen by those who were most closely involved in it as an event in which the God of Israel had shown himself more than ever to be the saviour and liberator of his people, in the most comprehensive and the most radical meaning of these terms. That was their interpretation, hesitantly begun at the time of their encounter with Jesus, and made definitive in their experiences of him after his death. The leaders of the Jewish community also knew Jesus and were aware of what he did and proclaimed, but they gave another interpretation of it on the basis of their faith, their relationship with God. In the picture which they made of Israel's God they could find no place for Jesus as a man through whom this God wanted to communicate something about himself.

For a Christian, to believe in God means that you take up the interpretation of Jesus by his first disciples and entrust yourself, in their footsteps, to the one who has made known his true nature in what Jesus did and what happened to him, and communicate it to you. In this he shows you that he accepts you unconditionally, as well, and is always ready to give you a new start. I put it in this way, because here I have begun to describe one of the starting points of those who told the stories about the birth of Jesus: the experiences of the creative force of God which makes things new, in their own lives and those of their fellow believers.

This is the way in which in their narratives they came to describe how Jesus had been fathered by the creative spirit.

We now put the question in this way: as a believing Christian, *must* you accept that *only this detail* from the group of stories around the birth of Jesus records a historical fact, the miracle of a conception which does not involve a man?

In the case of Jeremiah it was a question of public facts which could be seen and heard by bystanders, and the same thing is true in the case of Jesus' ministry. However, the conception of Jesus was related as an extremely intimate event, according to Luke known only to Mary, and according to Matthew also to Joseph; moreover the interpretation was already contained, included within it, 'by the holy Spirit'. Because there is no other reference to this intimate miracle elsewhere in the narratives and the proclamation of the New Testament, it seems to me the most honest thing to treat it in the same way as all the other details of the birth narratives, as a confession in story form of the new thing that God has begun for us in Jesus.

I have noted more than once that people were happy with this approach. For under the influence of all kinds of developments, in both church and society, at a very early stage, by the end of the second century, certain Christians had begun to regard sexual intercourse between man and woman, even in marriage, as sinful. They therefore believed that God would have kept the 'incarnation' of his son outside this sphere! Increasing veneration of the mother of Jesus also played a part in the conviction that as a holy woman she had abstained from intercourse with her husband. Sometimes it was even assumed that Mary had made a vow of virginity, so that her question to the angel Gabriel, 'How can this happen, as I know no man?', would refer to that. Fortunately it is clear that these ideas were inconceivable in the milieu of Joseph and Mary, and that they were also completely alien to Luke and Matthew.

I think, however, that in this connection another kind of 'must' is in place. Anyone who has adopted the approach I have described and is happy with it must be very careful in conversations with fellow Christians about the virginity of Mary and about the birth narratives as a whole. A deep reverence for the mother of God can be an essential part of a Roman Catholic's experience of faith. Furthermore, for a great many Christians the birth narratives as told by Luke and Matthew, with their unforgettable details, can be very closely bound up with celebrating Christmas and all that goes with it. For countless people who have long since stopped going to church, Christmas is still their one link with the Christian tradition. That is reason enough for being very careful about newly acquired insights into the real nature of the Christmas stories.

10 Praying

Training for the priesthood used to begin with a couple of years of philosophy. We learned how you had to define terms as accurately as possible before you used them in arguments. And these arguments had to be carried on in accordance with particular rules, otherwise they were invalid, illogical. After we had learned the laws of logic, we dealt with what lay behind tangible things, their existence, their being. But what is 'being'?

I remember that we always found that very difficult. One of us got a visit from his parents. He tried to explain to them what these lessons were about. He didn't succeed. So he resorted to an illustration: 'Philosophy is about a pipe without a bowl, the stem of which is missing.' That didn't seem to be too crazy. For what we were thinking about was not the properties of things, what makes things different from one another, but what they all have in common, namely their existence. They can lose that, in which case they no longer exist. They have existence, and they must have obtained it from something which did not need to obtain it, something that has existence in its own right and therefore cannot lose it: existence without limitations, in perfection. And that, we were told, is what all people call 'God'.

This argument became firmly fixed in my mind. When I heard or read the question 'Does God exist?', the answer came into my head automatically. But *you* exist. And if there were no God, you would not exist either!

However, I never said that out loud, although it was so evident to me. I was afraid that people would find it naive. Moreover; you can't say any more about this 'God'. We also learnt that in the lessons. That which exists of itself is unlimited. You cannot call it a something or a someone. For these are always limited entities, always a particular, circumscribed something or someone. That which exists of itself, 'God', cannot be described, cannot be grasped. You can only say something meaningful by adding 'not', saying what God is *not*.

That is the way we learned to think about being in our philosophy lessons. However, things were very different in church. We lived in a monastery. We gathered together to pray several times a day. The texts which we read and sang together were almost all from the Bible. In that book God is 'someone'. The people who wrote the Bible talked about God and to God as he, and him, and you. For them it went without saying that God was masculine. There is often mention of his face, his eyes, ears, nose and mouth, his arms and hands and feet. God also has a heart and innards from which his thoughts and plans and feelings come: love, joy, wrath, scorn. He once made 'heaven and earth', all that exists, what we call the universe. All this has been made by him. But he continues to be active in creation. Nothing escapes him. He is involved with everything that happens in that universe, and with every human being. Men and women can speak with God at any moment of their lives. For although God is conceived of in human terms, no matter what, he never sleeps.

Despite having these philosophy lessons at the back of our minds, we did not find the unsophisticated biblical talk about God strange or childish. Were we young men, of about twenty, not critical enough then? Or had the Bible, in that framework of centuries-old liturgical prayer, such authority over us that we took it in virtually without thinking, appropriated that talk about and to God without asking questions? Only much later did we begin to realize that the biblical language was by no means as naive as all that. For these people of the Bible certainly will have thought about it. In old stories they indeed depict God in a very human way. He takes clay, models it, shapes a human body and then breathes air into the nostrils. That is how he made the first man. When the flood is announced and Noah has brought a pair of each kind of animal into his great boat, the ark, God himself comes to shut the door tightly after him. Later God comes to visit Abraham, who has pitched his tent in the neighbourhood of Hebron: then he walks for a while with him eastwards, in the direction of the Dead Sea.

These old stories depict God in human terms, but in such a

way that there is no lack of reverence. God remains as it were full of majesty, quite different from the people with whom he deals. Yet the narrators sometimes feel the need to put a messenger, an 'angel', between God and the people he wants to encounter, someone who 'represents' him. This happens in the story in Judges 13: the couple who are to have the hero Samson as their son are visited by such an angel. He announces the birth of a child to the woman, who has hitherto been barren. After his departure, when it has become clear that he was the messenger of God, the father cries out in terror: 'Now we shall die, for we have seen God!'

This conviction is often expressed in the Bible. God is so highly exalted that anyone who sees him dies. At the same time people know that he is very near, involved in everything, and that he seeks a relationshp with people. Thus in Exodus 33 it is said of Moses that God spoke to him 'face to face, as a man speaks with his friend'. Directly after that there is another story in which God says to Moses, 'You cannot see my face, for no man can see me and live.' What Moses may see is something of the glory of God, a kind of dazzling glow. Moses has to go and stand in a hole in the rock when God passes by in this glow, and there God protects him with his hand. 'When I withdraw my hand you can see my back parts: my face you cannot see.'

God is very intimate, like a friend, and God is infinitely remote, as the one who is completely other, 'the Holy One', who may only be approached after a great deal of preparation. Among the Jews, emphasis began to be placed more and more on this latter aspect. Before the Babylonians made an end of the kingdom of Judah in 587 BC people could still talk about what King Hezekiah had done a century before. At that time the Assyrian armies were in process of conquering the cities of his small kingdom. They sent a message to Jerusalem that they also planned to seize the capital. Hezekiah read the letter, went into the innermost part of the temple, opened the letter there and said, 'Yahweh, behold their plan. What am I to do with this letter?' After the Babylonian exile such a thing became increasingly inconceivable, and not only because there was no longer a king and because the Judaeans who had returned formed a kind of religious community led by a high priest. It was inconceivable above all because the emphasis increasingly came to lie on the exalted nature and remoteness of Yawheh. The innermost part of the newly built temple was always closed in. Only once a year might the high priest enter it, after he had 'hallowed' himself in all kinds of ways. People also increasingly avoided pronouncing the proper name of Israel's God. In the old stories he had made known his name, Yahweh, because this was how he wanted to be addressed by his people; thus it was an indication of the intimacy which he desired. However, the sense of God's exaltedness became so dominant among the Jews that they no longer dared to speak this name aloud, and instead of it they would say, for example, 'the Lord'.

They even began to avoid the more general word 'God', replacing it with other expressions like heaven, the power, the name, the dwelling and so on. In some circles people were also fond of using the passive form to denote God's work. When they were talking about God's reaction to a good human deed, people could say, 'Heaven will reward you', or also, 'You will be rewarded'. The sense of God's exaltedness also meant that in their many prayers Jews came more to praise and thank him than to ask him for help in matters of daily life.

We also find that Jesus speaks reverently about God in this way. Like the other pious Jews he uses paraphrases. Just as a shepherd is glad when he has found a lost sheep, so there is 'joy in heaven' when a sinner repents. Jesus means: so God is happy that someone has returned to him. In his story of the prodigal son, Jesus makes the young man repeat on his way home what he will say to his father when they meet. 'Father, I have sinned "against heaven" and against you', instead of 'against God and against you'. He sometimes replaces the word God with 'the Most High' or 'the Lord of Heaven and Earth'. He often uses a passive to indicate something that God is doing or will do. As you judge men, he says, so you will be judged, that is, so God will judge you. The Most High and the supreme judge is also involved in caring for all that exists, that lives. He takes great pains in clothing the flowers of the field attractively, and he sees that even the smallest birds get food. No sparrow escapes his attention. After pointing this out to people, Jesus says, 'so the hairs of your head are numbered', i.e., so God has numbered the hairs of your head.

The striking thing about Jesus is that this reverential talk about

God went with an unprecedented familiarity in speaking to God. By that I mean his use of 'Abba', rather like 'Dear dad', or however young children affectionately address their father. It made such an impression that Greek-speaking disciples sometimes left this Aramaic word untranslated. The Jews certainly used *Abi* and *Abinu*, my father and our father, in Hebrew prayers, but when they did they usually added something like 'and our king', or 'who art in heaven'. Jesus simply said Abba, and wanted his disciples to address God in the same way. It was in Matthew's community that this simple form was expanded to 'Our Father who art in heaven'.

Each of the four evangelists tells us in his own way that Jesus often prayed. Sometimes he addressed God spontaneously when others were present. Often he withdrew into a solitary place in order to speak to his Father alone. But he often talked about prayer. He tried to make clear in the strongest possible terms that a person can always pray, can ask something of God, and that he will always be heard. I'm now thinking of the short tale in Luke 11, about the person who knocked on a friend's door one night. Here Jesus had in mind a house of the kind that I've often seen in the villages of what used to be Palestine: a dwelling with one room in which the whole family, father, mother and children, sleep on a raised part at the back, while in the front part there are sometimes domestic animals among the household goods and furniture. The door is shut from inside with a beam. The story also takes for granted that a guest is given a warm welcome, even if he comes at an inconvenient moment. As usual Jesus begins with a question, 'Which of you who has a friend will go to him at midnight and say to him, "Friend, lend me three loaves; for a friend of mine has arrived on a journey, and I have nothing to set before him"; and he will answer from within, "Do not bother me; the door is now shut, and my children are with me in bed; I cannot get up and give you anything?"' This story is really one long question: can you imagine that someone would react like this to a friend's request? It's inconceivable. So you mustn't worry about bothering God, who is much more concerned about you than your best friend!

In Luke this story is followed by a saying of Jesus about prayer which is given rather differently in Matthew 7, though also with a reference to what people usually do. First there is a threefold

138

exhortation: 'Ask and it shall be given to you, seek and you shall find, knock and it shall be opened to you,' in other words, 'God will open to you.' Then there is a threefold assurance: 'All those who ask receive, those who seek find, and those who knock have the door opened to them.' Then comes a question, 'Which father among you, when his son asks for bread will give him a stone, or if he asks for a fish, will give him a serpent?' The conclusion is, 'If you, who are evil, can give good gifts to your children, how much more will God your Father give good things to those who ask him for them?'

Note that Jesus evidently took it for granted that we human beings are evil – of course in comparison with God, who alone is utterly good, just as he once says to someone who addresses him as 'Good master', 'Do not call me good, for only God is good.' It was just as obvious to him that human fathers are good to their children.

Another of Jesus' stories connected with prayer comes in Luke 18. 'In a certain city there was a judge who neither feared God nor regarded man; and there was a widow in that city who kept coming to him and saying, "Vindicate me against my adversary." For a while he refused; but afterward he said to himself, "Though I neither fear God nor regard man, yet because this widow bothers me, I will vindicate her, or she will wear me out by her continual coming."' (We might translate the last phrase rather differently, as 'or she will make me lose face', get me talked about. This story is like that of the friend who is disturbed at night but still does as he is asked. However, it is much more vivid; if even a judge who does not respect God finally yields to the pressure of a poor widow, how much more will God accept the persistent cries of his people in need! Here Luke adds the question, 'When the Son of man comes, will he still find faith on earth?': for him, persistence in faith evidently implied that Christians should pray zealously for the promised consummation. In Jesus' prayer after the petition that God's name should be hallowed, that God should be recognized by all things and all men, the second clause was, 'Thy kingdom come'. For Christians, this would happen when Jesus was manifested as the glorified Son of man, at his coming or 'parousia'.

We can see from the book of Acts and from the letters of the apostles how important praying was for the first generation of

Christians. It has been observed that on this subject the vocabulary of the New Testament is richer than that of other Jewish writings from the same period.

In his own way, Paul, evidently from his own experience, gives the reasons for the new dimension which praying has taken on since the unprecedented manifestation of the creative spirit of God in Jesus. In chapter 4 of his letter to the Galatians he compares the earlier relationship of believers to God with that of servants, slaves, to their master. But, he says, 'when the fullness of time had come, God sent his son to free us from slavery, so that we too should have the status of sons. The evidence for that is that God has sent the spirit of his son into our hearts to cry "Abba, Father".' He goes into this in more detail in chapter 8 of his letter to the Romans: 'Only those who are led by the spirit of God are sons of God. For you have not received a spirit of slavery to live again in fear, but you have received the spirit of sonship, whereby we cry, "Abba, Father". The spirit itself bears witness of our spirit that we are children of God.' Those who are 'incorporated' into Christ by their belief and their baptism feel within themselves this urge to address God in the way that Jesus did. And a little further on, he says that we ourselves sometimes do not know precisely how to pray, but that in that case the spirit cries out in us with 'sighs that cannot be put into words'.

Thus the prayer of the first Christians is strongly influenced by what we can call their sense of newness, the certainty that God had come to meet man in a new and definitive way, by bringing about everything that used to go with the 'outpouring of the holy Spirit'. The Holy Spirit implanted in believers a fiery longing for the parousia, all the more because they had the certainty and often also the experience that before this they would still have to withstand much oppression. They prayed for the coming of the perfect kingdom of God, and at the same time for perseverance in the last and fiercest trials.

In later centuries, this expectation of a cosmic consummation faded into the background. But the New Testament texts about prayer continued to speak to Christians, who in all kinds of ways developed a 'culture of prayer'.

In our time many Christians have put question marks against this culture. That is also said by people who are still sufficiently attracted by 'the faith' to become involved in discussion groups. I am occasionally asked to take part in such a group on the evenings when they discuss biblical texts. I then listen to what is said about prayer. That subject also comes up at times when people want to talk to me about their experience of belief. In what follows I shall give a selection of what I've heard people say recently.

'God is too vague for me to be able to talk to him.' The Catholic writer Cornelis Verhoeven once put this difficulty sharply into words in the weekly journal *De Tijd*. Discussing a book about prayer he wrote that the subject was alien to him. Meditation, yes, he could manage that. 'Meditation is thinking inwardly and praying is talking to someone outside. Above all I have always found that precarious talking in the second person singular to someone who isn't there, or at least who doesn't reply, an unsurmountable problem.' What he went on to write could well apply to himself. 'I know at least one person who has been brought up to prayer, meditation and some practices which combine the two and who perhaps for that reason never gets off the ground in that area.' He ends: 'I continue to feel that a particular use of the second person singular is the real problem.'

Believers who have steeped themselves in the living faith of the people of the Bible, especially the writers of the Psalms, do not recognize that problem. They react rather like this: 'God is indeed everywhere and at work in everything. His creative breath blows on everything that lives. Should he stop breathing, everything would collapse. He also breathes life into you, you constantly receive it from him. How can you say that he is not there? He is the only one who is utterly there, in his own right, and is not dependent on something or someone else. And how can you claim that he doesn't answer back? He is the one who began by speaking and he has called everything, including you, into existence with the intention that we, and you too, should say something in reply.'

But is there not something artificial about putting yourself in the place of these people of former times, in a completely different culture? This culture was 'religious' through and through. Public life in antiquity was characterized by the worship of gods and goddesses, and all that went with it by way of temples, sacrifices, priests, festivals – you name it. That also influenced the thought-world and the feelings of the average citizen. The idea that God did not exist, or, as they would have had to put it, that the gods did not exist, could scarcely arise. The gods were part of their lives. Of course the Jews and Christians stood somewhat apart, with their belief in one God, which made them disown the existence of a multitude of gods, and which is why they were made out to be atheists. But they did not need to justify the fact that they believed in their one God and therefore spoke to him in the second person singular. Everybody did that; every religious person prayed in this way to his or her god or goddess.

In our society things are completely different. God and religion now have hardly any meaning in public life and in the life of the average citizen. God does not exist for people in the sense that they should take account of him in one way or another. That is the consequence of a development in our Western culture that I need not describe: God is no longer needed as an explanation of natural phenomena, we are aware that it's up to us to do things, and so on. It is now the case that for most people God does not exist, or at least has nothing to do with their own existence. Some people might perhaps say that something like a 'supreme being' exists. I recall that years ago I was once invited quite spontaneously to a meal by someone whom I barely knew. When we were about to eat, along with his wife and his son, he suddenly said, 'Oh, would you like to say grace?' And immediately afterwards he added, 'We don't normally. We don't want to bother the Supreme Being when we're going to eat some bread and butter.' God didn't exist for them as a personal presence, as someone with whom you have friendly relationships, who is interested in everything about you, even in the eating you may do to sustain the life which you receive from him.

If you do believe that God is 'personally' concerned for us, someone with whom you can talk, you go against what people generally feel. Verhoeven called such talk precarious, but did not make it clear why. Perhaps because it goes against rational thought, and therefore is risky, a danger to spiritual health?

By chance, in the same issue of *De Tijd* there was a piece about the diary by Etty Hillesum, which I have already mentioned. That book had made a very deep impression on some of those whom I encountered in groups or as individuals. They saw Etty Hillesum as a woman of our time who had also felt the precariousness of talking with God and yet found the courage to venture on it, to kneel down and say the name of God. She wrote: 'Some time ago I said to myself, I will practise kneeling. I'm still embarrassed about that gesture, which is as intimate as those loving gestures about which people can speak only if they are poets.' Her older friend S. had said to her some weeks before that people need to have courage to pronounce the name God. He said to Etty that it had been a long time before he had dared to do that. It was as if he still found something ridiculous in it, though he sometimes prayed for people. Then Etty asked, as unashamedly and cold-bloodedly as ever, 'What do you pray then?' 'And then a shyness came over him and this man who always gave a crystal clear answer to my most subtle and intimate questions said in some confusion, "I won't tell you, not now, later ..." '

If you read on, you will see Etty coming to a constantly deeper form of prayer. That goes hand in hand with a growing sense of God's activity in nature and in the flowers, in the universe, but above all it makes her increasingly sensitive to suffering in other people. She also refuses to have anything to do with expressions of hate against the Germans who are busy exterminating her people. So as a result of her conversation with God she too breaks out of the accepted patterns in her surroundings and thus becomes an outsider. If I remember rightly, in her diary she once repeats words of Jesus from the Gospels, but she never mentions him by name. She only reports what her older friend had said on his death bed: 'I dreamed that Christ baptized me.'

Yes, someone might say, but this Etty was an exception. That's true. The way in which she came to talk to God, the 'apocalyptic' circumstances in which this conversation developed, her need to write about this intimate relationship, and at the same time her poetic sense that no words are really adequate to describe the deepest experiences, all this is quite exceptional, including the fact that her intimate writings were published. Moreover, although her diary has gone through many printings in Holland, even those who buy it and those who have the time and the sense to read it are an exception, a tiny privileged minority.

But why should there not be a lot of people who respond to God like Etty, and in the same way also develop a deep humanity and with it a great concern for their fellow human beings? Why shouldn't they do this as a matter of course, so that they need not think deeply about it and need not feel they have to talk about it? However, you don't meet such people in discussion groups!

In such groups it is often observed that the way in which Christians are brought up to pray has been wrong. As a child you had to say prayers, morning and evening, grace before meals, and you had to go to church, where you heard and said all sorts of things which had no connection with what you were thinking and feeling yourself. Was Verhoeven thinking of this pressure when he wrote about those ' who were brought up in these things and perhaps for that reason never get off the ground in that area'. At all events, many people say that it is precisely the fact that they *had* to pray which made them stubbornly resist. What they had to say had no connection with their own feelings or what they found important when they became adolescents. It has been observed that English has two different words for German *Glaube* and Dutch *geloof*, faith and belief. People understand by faith a complex of truths and rules of life, whereas belief denotes what you value from inside, truth which you accept. It is said that our parents taught us 'faith', a whole series of clear answers to questions that we did not raise. And we could not get answers from them to our real questions. Their faith provided them with no reply. This criticism has also been put like this. Many people have experiences that you could call religious, real experiences of God. They can suddenly feel overwhelmed by something that transcends them, almost terrifyingly great yet at the same time fascinating. This grandeur can be something in nature, something that reduces you to silent wonderment; or it can be a work of art, or the wonder of a love which comes into being between two people. But in our youth 'God' was put in a separate compartment; he belonged to 'religion' which was regarded specifically as an unpleasant obligation. We did not learn to look on such deep experiences in a religious way, as manifestations of the mysterious reality in and behind all things which is called God. In place of prayers and formulas which meant nothing to us, we should really have learned how to become sensitive to these manifestations, even 'revelations' of the divine to us.

Does that mean being brought up to be people who are really alive? Yes, that is what was really meant. Everyone has deep within himself or herself an area which is open to that mysterious element, that all-embracing reality. However, for many Westerners the way to it has become obstructed. That is evident from our life-style, which in turn we hand on to our children as we bring them up. Everyone is in a hurry, rushing from one thing to another, failing to give themselves the time and leisure to let impressions sink in. They think of what's coming next, something else to be done, to be experienced. The view of imposing mountain scenery cannot be a deep experience if you are sitting in a speeding car or busy on a picnic or thinking about the chances of going climbing in those mountains next year. You need inner rest and quietness to be touched to the depths. And that is also true of contacts with fellow human beings. Other people who want to make contact with you notice well enough when that's impossible, when you're not with them although you may be sitting there. You're preoccupied with other things. Your attention is not with this other person; you're distracted, busy with all kinds of things somewhere else. To be able to concentrate our attention is part of the art of real living, from deep down within ourselves. It's also called being able to live in the here and now. We're not trained for that.

Perhaps connected with this is another characteristic of our Western European way of life. People, especially men, find it hard to cope with their feelings. It is impressed on them that they must control their feelings; it's wrong for a man to show violent emotions. He must be rational, matter-of-fact. In this way people can become afraid of their own feelings and unconsciously develop techniques to defuse them. That too reduces the possibility of our being affected by experiences which we could call religious, and also of our sharing them with others who are open to them.

That all this is bound up with our difficulties over praying was made particularly clear to me during my stay in African countries. The missionary sisters who were my real responsibility introduced me to the way in which their Christians expressed their faith. Time and again I noticed how open the simple villagers were, how authentic and intense was their way of life, how their hearts were always in what they said and did. I sometimes thought how close they were to their 'source'! Life flowed in and through them. In the utmost poverty, they showed an intense joy in life, which was also expressed in their warm hospitality, their delight in sharing the little they had.

They could sing and dance together in church, and in the intercessions could lay their needs before God the Father without any confusion or shame. If a man or a woman was praying in this way, you could feel that the others were not just listening quietly and reverently, but were also involved in what he or she was saying to God and were utterly caught up in it. More than once I found myself asking what we Westerners really have to contribute when it comes to the quality of life.

Recently, one of those who wanted to tell me how she herself felt about praying was a teacher in her late twenties. As a child she had been against grace before and after meals. That was the custom in the family of her Christian parents. One day she had refused to say grace with them. But she noted at that time how she was often talking to God during the day. God, isn't that beautiful? God, why did it happen? When I asked whether that had not been a kind of expletive, she said, 'No, I've thought about that. I express my feelings, important things about myself, the suffering of others which affects me, and even my rebelliousness. Sometimes I quarrel with him. It's all prayer to me. First of all I thought that it wasn't praying, because it happened without fixed words, and wasn't at fixed times and places. It wasn't even pious. That word had negative overtones for me: being brave, raising eyes to heaven to glorify God. But now that's the way I pray. Whenever I feel deep down in myself and that feeling brings me close to other people, then I'm praying.'

She had a deep antipathy to formal prayers. She had only recently started going to church again, to ecumenical services, and also taking part in them, as a reader. 'When I have to do the intercessions I never say, "Let us pray", but "Let us try to pray", or better, 'Let us first keep silence", because you can't pray just like that. I know that of old, when I had too much of it. If you want to keep in contact with God then you mustn't let yourself be distracted. If you're distracted, you can't really be deeply concerned for yourself and others. So you must develop moments of quietness, create spaces for them in your life.' Thus despite her antipathy to 'regimented' prayer and her criticism of the church where 'everything has to be so neat', she also saw the need for regular times to be alone and still, since otherwise it was impossible to feel deeply or pray authentically.

These ecumenical services had also attracted her because the participants voiced their concerns, in their own lives and outside this circle. She told me with some emotion of the sympathy for the three black men in South Africa who had been condemned to death, and how they prayed for them and their families when they were hanged. One reason for ending with this story is to show that praying does make sense.

I was surprised to hear how this woman found it quite natural to combine two essential features of Christian prayer. On the one hand was her striving for silence, inner stillness, in order to get near to the 'core', the deepest 'self', that point of contact with the mystery of being, 'God'. On the other hand was her realization that this most individual encounter with God gets its social dimension in common prayer, particularly in the eucharist. Eating and drinking what Christ offers us, his 'life', we experience our 'corporate' living in him, and so our communion with each other and with other human beings in need, far away. Thus a living faith brings us nearer both to our deepest self and to all those with whom we share our humanity.

11 Unpretentious Preaching

A letter

Dear Ton,

In your modest way you asked for the text of the sermon that I was toiling over when you telephoned. You had heard me preaching in the service which had been televised from Amersfoort and you were interested in what I was going to say on Ascension Day. If you weren't already aware of the fact, you will have seen from that television broadcast that a sermon does not have the same function for us Roman Catholics as it does for you members of the Reformed Church. For you it is the main item in the Sunday service, and the sermon must above all be the interpretation of a biblical text, the Word of God. The preacher is a 'Minister of the Word' and this is what church people, who are themselves brought up on the Bible, expect of him. For us Roman Catholics, the sermon is only a minor element in the service. It is part of the introduction to the main event, the celebration of the last supper, the eucharist. The biblical texts which are read aloud during the introduction are appointed for each Sunday in the official order of service, the so-called Roman Missal. There are always three of them: a passage from one of the Gospels, preceded by a piece from the Old Testament chosen in connection with that Gospel, along with another passage from one of the New Testament letters or the Acts of the Apostles. The preacher is not expected to preach for more than ten to fifteen minutes. You can imagine how for days beforehand I keep thinking about what I have to say and how I'm going to say it, and how I spend the whole of Saturday working away in order to get my text ready!

You will say: Luke, of course I can understand that. The time is much too short to expound even one of these three texts properly, so that its message comes over clearly to people. You've devoted the best years of your life to the study of the Bible, and if you want to bring out everything that you can find in one bit of text, then you need a great deal more time! That's certainly part of the problem, Ton, but there's another reason why I find my preparation so disturbingly difficult. The main reason is that I can see before me all the people to whom I'm going to speak, and they're all so different. There are older people who've gone through a great deal; perhaps a husband or wife has died, or there's been a divorce. I can think of a couple whose ten-year-old son was killed while he was playing. Rather younger people may be looking for a meaning in life and may even be on the verge of leaving the church, like the student who said to me: 'I really can't take any more of it, being talked at for a whole hour.'

I also think of all the arrangements these people with families keep having to make in order to be able to get to church on time. In that connection I often remember a teacher who once told me after the twelve o'clock service: 'I just made it after seeing my wife in the clinic, where she's recovering from her operation; then immediately afterwards I go at visiting time to the hospital nearby to visit our oldest boy. He's gone in there again because of his congenital heart disease.'

That makes me think: Luke, who are you to dare to talk to these people, with your comfortable life in a monastery? You have no worries about money and no problems about getting enough to eat; you live in an atmosphere which is hardly marked by shared commitment. You're celibate, without a wife. You miss the joys of marriage, but you also miss the struggle and the pain; you've no children, and while you miss the riches they bring, you also escape the vulnerability. You're so far removed from the experiences that make up the lives of your congregation. Now I can hear you telling me, Ton, that I don't preach myself to people but the word of God, and that's my real task. Yes, that's true, and a Catholic could also add that I have been solemnly ordained for my ministry by the bishop, to function as a priest, and that preaching is also part of that ministry. But I have to confess that my feelings aren't helped much by these fine words: minister of the word, ordained to this priesthood.

They are not what give me courage to speak in church. As I see it, there's only one reason why I dare to do that. I have been allowed more time to spend on the study of the Bible and to reflect a bit on our faith. This knowledge helps me to clarify things, to explain them to people. When I used to celebrate regularly in the student church here, I found a comparison helpful in explaining this. A group of people want to go to look at a famous painting in a museum. An art historian tells them a few things, about the painter and his techniques, and then points out all kinds of details in the painting which the onlookers might otherwise have missed. After that he goes off and leaves them alone with the work of art. Then their real encounter with the painting begins, and they are all free to let it make its own impression on them, to affect them in their own way.

That's how I see my task as a preacher: on the basis of my knowledge I can point out a few details in a biblical text, or an aspect of belief; sometimes, too, I can show its connection with the celebration of the eucharist which is to follow – and that rite is also full of meaning – then I disappear into the group, leaving the people (and myself) alone, each with his or her own approach, with his or her own way of being affected by what is presented to us in pictures and symbols.

So there is no 'socio-political involvement' in my sermons. No. During that period of preaching in the student church to which I referred earlier, I was asked several times to discuss the theme of theme of 'Israel: people, land and state'. People knew how much I was at home in that subject and how much I was also affected by it. I always flatly refused. I felt that that would be to abuse my position of power. I certainly won't talk on a disputed subject to several hundred people who can't say anything in reply. Certainly more than once at the end of a sermon I've said that I would like to discuss the question after the service over coffee. A number of churchgoers have come up and we have had vigorous, often emotional exchanges, but at all events they were honest, and on an equal footing.

It would be quite different if I had to preach every week, as the pastor of a parish, to people whom I knew personally, whose joys and sorrows I could share. But even then, I think, I would not introduce any controversial subjects of a political nature into a church service. I would do that in another context, in open

150

discussions. In sermons I would repeat in all kinds of ways that to live as a Christian, in the spirit of Christ, essentially implies that people should be politically active, make choices, and that a churchgoer who does not do this is in fact supporting the *status quo*.

However, I personally find talking together about aspects of our faith far more attractive than giving a monologue – which is what a sermon really is. What I like most of all is discussing biblical texts in a small group. Each person contributes the fruits of his or her own quiet reading and tranquil contemplation on parts of the biblical text which have appealed to them. I do the same thing, and then of course I say what I've learned about the text through study, for that has become a part of myself. In this way, in conversations, it's easier to get over the real purpose of well-known stories, like those about the birth of Jesus or about his appearances after Easter. In a sermon it's particularly difficult – which is one of the reasons why I sweat so much over them – not to perplex or to shock people, but to give them an insight which contributes to their confidence and their joy in life. Becuase that's what matters.

I've written all this, Ton, to explain to you why these sermons take the form they do.

Warmest greetings,
   Lucas

The first reading in the liturgy, from Colossians 1, includes the following passage:

> He is the image of the invisible God, the firstborn of all creation, for in him all things were created, in heaven and on earth, visible and invisble... all things were created through him and for him. He is before all things and in him all things hold together.

Second reading: Luke 23.35-43

> When Jesus was hanging on the cross the people stood by, watching; but the rulers scoffed at him, saying, 'He saved others, let him save himself, if he is the Christ of God, his Chosen One!' The soldiers mocked him, coming up and offering him vinegar, and saying, 'If you are the king of the Jews, save yourself!' There was also an inscription over him, in letters of Greek and Latin and Hebrew, 'This is the king of the Jews.' One of the criminals who were hanged railed at him, saying, 'Are you not the Christ? Save yourselves and us!' But the other rebuked him, saying, 'Do you not fear God, since you are under the same sentence of condemnation? And we indeed justly; for we are receiving the due reward of our deeds; but this man has done nothing wrong.' And he said, 'Jesus, remember me when you come in your kingly power.' And he said to him, 'Truly, I say to you, today you will be with me in paradise.'

We have listened to two passages from the New Testament, and it will certainly have struck you what a great difference there is between them. First in form: the last passage was a narrative, an account of Jesus on the cross. The first passage, from Paul included a song of praise to this same Jesus who is before all things, in all things, the head of all things. God's fullness dwells in him.

The difference between these two texts becomes even greater

when we imagine what the first readers felt and knew. Death on the cross was at that time the most abhorrent, the cruellest death imaginable. The Romans reserved this punishment for people who were a danger to the state, rebels. And in Jesus' case, the Jewish authorities had in fact handed him over because he was disobedient to the law, and therefore really a rebel. Then there was this group of people in Colossae. In his letter Paul uses a song of praise that they sang there. These people, thousands of miles away in Asia Minor, were quite crazy about this Jesus and went into raptures about him in their song, 'He, he is the image of the invisible God, in him all things are created, all that exists. He is the firstborn from the dead, the head of all peoples.' And you could ask the question – keeping on asking questions is a weakness of mine – how did it happen that people came to worship an outcast who had been tortured to death as the centre, the head of all creation? I shall try to answer this question in a few words which may be of some help. I think that perhaps this Jesus treated people in such a way that they again had a sense of the creator; Jesus dealt creatively with people, and that stood out. For he was a Jew, and it's worth remembering that in the world of the time, the word Jew was synonymous with 'one God, one Creator and Lord of all', since all other people throughout the Roman world believed in a whole series of gods and goddesses and powers and forces, and only the Jews said, 'No, there is only one.' And they knew that they had been taken into the confidence of this one God. He had made a covenant with them, and they alone knew what reality was really like. Moreover, he had given them a law for living in such a way that they remained within that covenant, within that trusting relationship with God. They had laws, rules of life, customs which set them apart from all other peoples. And they were grateful for this certainty. They were proud of the trust that had been placed in them, and they found it a good thing in this confused human world to know precisely with whom one should mix and whose company one should avoid. Of course they had no dealings with Jews who broke the law, or with people who were clearly afflicted by God like the sick and the lepers and the possessed – and of course they couldn't have any dealings at all with non-Jews. Jesus was a passionate Jew. More than others, I feel, he experienced this one God as creator. Not as someone who had once created, at one point, but as someone who is now creatively active in his world. This God is the one who carefully clothes the flowers and is interested in the birds; he is concerned for the sparrows and he is also passionately interested in all human beings, to whom he continues to give the gift of life, in the hope that they will share it out, that they will not keep this gift to themselves, will not hoard it or hide it away. That is the way in which Jesus lived out his own life, as given by the Creator. He spoke to him, dear people, he addressed him with greater familiarity than any Jew before him, calling him Abba, rather like 'dear Father'. And he thought, if only people would begin to live like that, sharing out their lives as a gift, then the old dream of the kingdom of God would become the reality of a completely new society.

This had begun in Jesus himself, and his lifework was to be to win people for it. But that appeared to be difficult. Most people were not free for it: most of them were imprisoned, as we can well imagine, in patterns of thought and action, in certainties, in securities which they did not want to lose. Jesus, you tell us to give away everything we have, but where does that get us? 'But that's the only way you can enter the kingdom of God,' says Jesus.

To be open to everyone, to accept everyone, to give to everyone, surely that cannot be? Look, this man clearly breaks the law, he's a sinner, and this woman, I don't need to tell you what she is.

'Do not judge,' says Jesus. God gives his good rain to the pious and sinners alike, without looking to see whether they deserve it. If you give like this, then you are a child of this Father.

Forgiving someone who does you wrong is all very well, Jesus, but surely you can't keep on doing that. You can't do it indefinitely. Yes, says Jesus, keep on doing that, for God does the same. Forgiving means offering a clean sheet, giving someone a new start, time and again. That's God's way of dealing creatively with people. Not pinning them down to something from the past, not pinning them down to what they've done, even if it was only yesterday.

Jesus had the gift of healing, and he used it to illustrate what that meant; he freed people from what had pinned them down, sickness, possession, leprosy, and in this way he gave them a new start. He preferred to do that on the sabbath. 'But surely you realize that such things aren't allowed on the sabbath?' they said. You know the law of God.' 'I know it very well,' said Jesus, 'and I can sum up the whole of God's law for you in a single sentence: do for others what you would want them to do for you.' That is the revelation of God. Jesus enjoyed life and he very much liked to celebrate this creative love of God at the table. He often sat at table and laughed a lot, at parties. He kept company with people who were open to his message and shared food and drink with them, the support for this gift of life. Eating and drinking together was a profound thing, and Jesus ate and drank with people who had been labelled publicans and sinners. Once he allowed his feet to be washed and anointed by a woman, a grateful woman, who had the reputation of being a prostitute.

In this way Jesus was occupied in creating new situations, breaking through all kinds of fixed patterns, fatalities like sickness and death. I'm always reminded of him by a well known hymn in which Huub Oosterhuis sings about the ways in which God is working, 'breaking with fate and embarking on new paths, and his hands involved in any new beginning'. I'd like to say a good deal more about Jesus' life, but there just isn't time. His creativity, the way he broke through established patterns, was unacceptable to the guardians of the established order. They had to shut him up, so they killed him, for that too is a law: 'Death shuts people up for good,' they thought. Isn't that so? When you're dead, you're dead.

However, this pattern too was broken. Jesus' death brought him even closer to God and therefore closer to people than before. This new human family then saw that kingdom of God for which he lived very clearly indeed – it took shape in groups of people, spreading further and further afield, who began to live together creatively in the spirit of Jesus, who made a new beginning. There were no more labels as there used to be, Jew and non-Jew, slave, freeman, scholar, ordinary person, man, woman – everybody was a human being. With their new role and their new life-style, they sang about this Jesus, 'God has made a new beginning in him.' He is the firstborn from the dead. Yes, he was already in God's mind when he began his creation. In him and for him everything has been created.

And so, dear people, we are back with the singing Colossians, and with ourselves, for today we are celebrating Christ as king. That means that in his spirit, under his leadership, we are trying to be creative with our lives and with one another. We want constantly to break through fixed patterns and not to succumb to fatalism, to thinking that things have to be like that, to situations where we think that there is nothing we can do. Each of you can think of something on a personal level: perhaps it's a personal relationship that's got stuck, or being confronted with a fatal illness. And on the world scale, there are the great threats which nothing seems to ward off, which seem constantly to come closer.

To support and inspire one another to be creative in all these situations is what I think being the church is about.

We will soon be invited to his table, just like those publicans and sinners. It means that he wants to be creative with us. That communion means for each of us the offer of a new start, no more of yesterday, no more of the past; a new start, now. And so Jesus remains as regal as the evangelist Luke told us a moment ago. For all that terrible pain on the cross, he remained attentive enough to listen to that man next to him longing for a new beginning, repenting. He responded in a very royal way. 'Not later, when I come again, but today, you shall be with me in paradise.' Amen.

Yesterday I had my sister on the telephone. When I said that I had to preach today she asked, 'Do you know the old Jewish story about the cow?' 'No,' I said. 'Well,' she went on, 'there was a rabbi who was not very well off, but he did have one cow. He got to know a family that was very poor, and he gave away his cow to these people. His children asked him what had happened to the cow. He told them that it had gone to heaven.' That's very profound, very Jewish: what you give to the poor goes to God. That's roughly what the story means. And we know this notion from our New Testament, which is a Jewish book. The Gentile Cornelius, a Roman officer, gave a lot away to poor people. One noontide he had a vision; an angel came to him, and when he seemed afraid the angel said, 'Your alms have ascended to God.'

It would be worth thinking a bit more about this today. If something that is completely given away to others goes to God, then we can use this idea to approach the mystery that we're celebrating: Jesus who had given himself completely, went to God, he went to heaven.

But the liturgy today offers us two texts which require us to listen carefully. They come from one writer, Luke, the only evangelist to relate the ascension of Jesus. He ends his first book, his Gospel, with the story, and then he begins his second book, Acts, with it, but the accounts are rather different. We shall look at those differences and in that way see what these stories really try to say about this ascension; then we can all rejoice over it together. Let us pray to God to help us understand his salvation in our life.

Before the reading of the Gospel

Before we begin to listen to Luke's accounts I want first to remind you of a few of his characteristics as a writer. First of all he was a man of his time and culture, not of ours. Then he was a very careful storyteller. Thirdly, he was a man of the church, in other words, he put his gifts as a writer at the service of the believing community of his church.

He was a man of his time. Some of you have experienced something of its culture at the grammar school; you may have read some of these 'classical' writers. Do you remember Livy, and what he says about the first king of the city of Rome? His name was Romulus. One day this king assembled the whole people before the walls of the city. The question was how many of them could fight in the army. Suddenly a terrible thing happened. A pitch-dark cloud descended on King Romulus. When the cloud lifted, he was no longer there. The people were at a loss, bewildered; then they began to rejoice: Romulus had now become a deity, 'father' of the city of Rome.

This is one story from many of its time. This was the way in which people stressed the greatness of particular individuals: they did not die in the ordinary way, but were transported, taken up. Luke knew of such stories from his culture, and also from the Jewish Bible. The greatest prophet, Elijah, did not die in the ordinary way but was transported to heaven in a fiery chariot.

Enoch, too, was transported by God. As you know, he was the seventh of the series of old men between Adam and Noah. Enoch's son Methusaleh was 969 years old, if you please. Enoch, the father, was only 365. He did not die in the ordinary way, this man who 'walked with God', but was taken up. Among the Jews there were stories in circulation about how that happened. He was talking to his followers when it suddenly became pitch dark: angels took him, and when it became light again he was no longer there.

Luke was familiar with this model. And he chose it to end his Gospel. With everyone else he believed that after his death Jesus lived with God, and he also knew of his appearances. If you're a careful storyteller you don't just describe someone's arrival and what he or she does – you also describe their departure. Just think of the splendid story of the angel's message. First Luke introduces the figures involved, then the angel arrives, then there is that unforgettable conversation which Mary brings to an end with her 'Be it to me according to your word,' and then, Luke writes, 'Then the angel departed from her'. That's how he wanted to end his first book, the Gospel, with Jesus' departure. The Risen Lord appeared to the disciples on the road to Emmaus, then on the evening of this Easter Day to the eleven apostles. After he had eaten something before their very eyes he gave them his last instructions and their commission, and then took them with him to the Mount of Olives, on which Bethany lies. Note how he blessed them, something he had never done in his earthly life, and how they fell down and worshipped him, which had never happened before. When he was taken up, they began to praise God in the temple, the place where Luke made his Gospel begin. Now let us listen reverently to the end of Luke's Gospel.

First reading: Luke 24.46-53

> On Easter Day he said to them: 'Thus it is written, that the Christ should suffer and on the third day rise from the dead, and that repentance and forgiveness of sins should be preached in his name to all nations, beginning from Jerusalem. You are witnesses of these things. And behold, I send the promise of my Father upon you; but stay in the city, until you are clothed with power from on high.'
> Then he led them out as far as Bethany, and lifting up his hands he blessed them. While he blessed them, he parted from them. And they returned to Jerusalem with great joy, and were continually in the temple blessing God.

Before the reading of Acts

Luke was a man of his time and culture, a careful narrator, but he was also and above all a man of the church, someone who put his own gifts as a writer at the service of the community of believers. So he begins his second book, Acts, with the ascension of Jesus, now with rather different accents and details. For he is writing in the 80s, half a century after Jesus' death, fifty years later. Even then there were still Christians who believed and hoped that the so-called parousia, the glorious return of the glorified son of man, would happen very soon. You will know that the expectation of a final 'coming' of God was alive among many Jews in the time of Jesus. Jesus, too, was full of this expectation, and the first generation of Christians were even more ardent, seeing him as the Son of man who would be coming soon. Paul expected that he himself would be involved in the end. Christians from Judaism expressed this in their own way. When the Son of man came, world rule would be given to the faithful of Israel, the saints of the Most High. He would restore the kingdom of Israel.

Luke now describes the ascension again, above all with an eye to these Christians. At the same time it enables him to give the programme of his book. The time when that glorious end will come, he tells people, has been determined only by God, who has told no one else. We cannot know it. But it is certainly not coming soon. For God is concerned not only with Israel but with the whole world, all nations, so it is your task to bear witness to him before all these Gentiles. So don't stand staring into heaven in expectation of Jesus' return, but go to work to preach the message of redemption and salvation in all lands, to the ends of the earth. And do that on the basis of the apostles' witness. That's really safe. For the Risen Jesus gave them further instruction for a whole forty days. On that basis go out into the world and be assured that he will certainly return to complete everything.

Second reading: Acts 1.1-11

In the first book, O Theophilus, I have dealt with all that Jesus began to do and teach, until the day when he was taken up, after he had given commandment through the Holy Spirit to the apostles whom he had chosen. To them he presented himself alive after his passion by many proofs, appearing to them during forty days, and speaking of the kingdom of God. And while staying with them he charged them not to depart from Jerusalem, but to wait for the promise of the Father, which, he said, 'you heard from me, for John baptized with water, but before many days you shall be baptized with the Holy Spirit.'

So when they had come together, they asked him, 'Lord, will you at this time restore the kingdom to Israel?' He said to them, 'It is not for you to know times or seasons which the Father has fixed by his own authority. But you shall receive the power when the Holy Spirit has come upon you; and you shall be my witnesses in Jerusalem and in all Judea and

160

Samaria and to the end of the earth.' And when he had said this, as they were looking on, he was lifted up, and a cloud took him out of their sight. And while they were gazing into heaven as he went, behold, two men stood by them in white robes, and said, 'Men of Galilee, why do you stand looking into heaven? This Jesus, who was taken up from you into heaven, will come in the same way as you saw him go into heaven.'

Meditation

What a difference there is between these two stories! The first takes place on Easter evening, the second forty days later. In the first Jesus blesses the disciples, in the second he doesn't. In the first there is no cloud, nor do two people in white garments come to speak to the disciples. Moreover, what Jesus himself says is very different.

You might want to say to Luke, 'That's all very well, but precisely what did happen, when did it happen, and precisely what did Jesus say then?'

I think that Luke would first of all be bewildered at these questions. For he was a man of his time and culture. But then perhaps he would say, 'Dear people, try to understand one thing: the *real* fact of Jesus' ascension *cannot* be described. His going to the Father, to heaven, happened on the cross, when he died. At that moment of extreme forsakenness, when his life was completely ruined, utterly shattered, at that very moment God's world opened up before him and he was taken up into the bosom of his Father, permeated by his life, recreated by his spirit. That was the real moment of his ascension. But that going of Jesus to the Father could not be seen by anyone, and therefore it could not be described. That falls outside our space and time. That can be experienced only in faith.'

What could be described were the experiences of the disciples which they called the 'appearances', and the way in which they were seized by the spirit, this divine power which had also driven Jesus on. Those were certainly facts within our space and time. But at the same time they were very mysterious. Luke's fellow evangelist John makes Jesus say to Mary Magdalene as early as Easter morning, 'I am ascending to my Father and your

Father.' On the evening of the same day he makes Jesus breathe on his disciples and say to them, 'Receive the Holy Spirit'. In John, both Ascension and Pentecost happen on Easter Day.

The ancient church celebrated them in that way for centuries: there was just one Easter mystery which embraced Ascension and Pentecost. Only in the fifth century did these become separate feasts, on the basis of Luke who chose the fortieth and fiftieth days for them.

However, there is also a good side to celebrating Ascension so separately. It stimulates us to think about the essence of it. Who was this man who was taken up to God in this way at his death? He was the one who had lived so utterly from God, always receiving his life consciously from God's hand; he rejoiced in that fact with a deep joy, and therefore he could give without anxiety or concern for himself; he let the stream flow unhindered to others; therefore he was harsh and fierce in his condemnation of everything that deprived people of it, wounded them, isolated them, set them apart, even when that happened in the name of God, indeed precisely when that happened in the name of God. He remained faithful to this concern for us men and women through the most cruel suffering that was inflicted on him, faithful even to death. We celebrate the fact that this man has gone to be with his God and our God, and invites us, urges us, through his spirit to live as he did, coming from God and going to God. So it is thanks to him that we can know the meaning of our existence and through his spirit may base our lives on him from whom we come and to whom we go. Although the name Jesus does not occur in the hymn we are going to sing, it is in his spirit.

Feast of the Holy Trinity

First Reading: Exodus 34.4b-6, 8-9

So Moses rose early in the morning and went up on Mount Sinai, as the Lord had commanded him, and took in his hand two tables of stone. And the Lord descended in the cloud and stood with him there, and proclaimed the name of the Lord. The Lord passed before him, and proclaimed, 'The Lord, the Lord, a God merciful and gracious, slow to anger, and abounding in steadfast love and faithfulness.' And Moses made haste to bow his head toward the earth, and worshipped. And he said, 'If now I have found favour in thy sight, O Lord, let the Lord, I pray thee, go in the midst of us, although it is a stiff-necked people; and pardon our iniquity and our sin, and take us for thine inheritance.'

Gospel: John 3.16-18

For God so loved the world that he gave his only Son, that whoever believes in him should not perish but have eternal life. For God sent the Son into the world, not to condemn the world, but that the world might be saved through him. He who believes in him is not condemned; he who does not believe is condemned already, because he has not believed in the name of the Son of God.

In Athens the apostle Paul once addressed a group of Greeks. He said this to them about God: He is not far from each one of us, for in him we live and move and have our being.

Here Paul seems to be expressing something that has always been sensed by people everywhere: our life is supported and at the same time surrounded by a reality which transcends us, 'God'. All religions are expressions of this sense. All religions are attempts to respond to this reality, to recognize it in community and to live in harmony with it.

Recently there has been a good deal of public interest in other religions. Makers of TV programmes and publishers are well

163

aware of it. Last night at eleven o' clock you could have looked at a programme on Hinduism. A few years ago the book of the month was called *Answer*, with the subtitle, 'Forms of Faith in Today's World'.

Those who make a really close study of other religions begin to see the character of our own more clearly. You could say that Christianity is characterized by personal relationships: God is Father, Son and Spirit and we respond to him as a community. I would like to share some reflections with you on the way in which that has gradually become clear. Then, of course, we end up with a question: Why is there a creation? Why are we here? Why am I here? We shall just touch on this question, and then, to end with I shall tell you what a child said to a wise priest.

That God is three was discovered, made manifest, quite slowly. The mystery which supports us and enfolds us was experienced by ancient Israel as a Someone. He was moved by the misery of a group of slaves in Egypt. He saved them from going under and made them his people. So he entered into a relationship with them, began a history with them.

You will have just noticed, in the story about Moses, how God describes himself in terms of a relationship: he is *hanun*, giving favours like a prince, but not from above, cool and remote, for in the first place he is *rahum*, emotionally involved, compassionate – the word has to do with 'womb', i.e. with motherly feelings. He is long-suffering, slow to be angry, not immediately cross when he is hurt. He has an abundant sense of community and faithfulness. That is how God describes himself, in terms of relationship, that is how he is for his people.

However, he also requires a response from his partner. We often hear how much he desired that. 'I had hoped that you would say Father to me and that you would behave as my devoted son.' But only a few people did that. Then Jesus came. He certainly behaved as a son. He saw his Father's breath of life at work in every flower, every bird, in the same way as the author of Psalm 104 saw God at work. Jesus also saw him as being full of concern for everyone, for every hair on their heads. But above all, Jesus responded to the Father by also being open to all men: gracious and merciful and longsuffering, and with an abundant sense of community and faithfulness – even to the point of death. Then his Father remained faithful to him, and

164

renewed him through his life-giving spirit. The spirit also renewed all those who believed in him and this gave rise to a new people of God, the church.

Christians were very aware of this: in this Jesus God has not sent us just one more prophet, someone with a message about him; no, in Jesus he has sent us what was always the most intimate part of himself, his Son, as much part of himself as his life-breath, his Spirit. And so Christians arrived at the conviction that their God is not solitary, all alone in his majesty, but consists in relationships, Father, Son and Spirit, an inconceivable intensity of total giving and total receiving. God is self-sufficient, completely happy.

And so I come to the second point: a question. Why did he then make the world with us in it, you and me? Not because he was alone and needed company. No, there can be only one reason: he wanted to give away his happiness. He wanted to share it. That is why he set in motion that powerful process of evolution which led up to humanity, organisms so sensitive and refined that they do not just react to stimuli from outside, but are aware of themselves, of an 'I' that can say 'you' to another I, and 'Thank you' to God.

Here God took a risk, the risk that a man would not give that answer, the risk of love.

Can you honestly think of anything like this? Can you imagine it? Someone once pointed out how it might be possible among human beings. Think of a truly happy family: the parents live in harmony with each other and with their children, in true mutual love. They are touched by the misery of a waif and resolve to take it into their family. At that moment they make their happiness partly dependent on that child. When it's out, and doesn't come home, they are anxious. When it is rebellious and goes its own way, they feel that too. Beforehand they were self-sufficient, but now to some extent they have put their happiness in the hands of the child.

Can we think of God a bit like that, that to some extent he has put his happiness in the hands of men and women? Yes, we can. For Jesus also thought that, and said it very clearly. When someone turns to God, that makes God happy: just like this woman who lost a coin and found it again; just like this shepherd who found the sheep that had got lost; just like this father when his prodigal son returned to him.

Jesus says this: you can make God happier when you turn to him in prayer for forgiveness, in praise and thanksgiving. To be aware of this and to put it into practice can give value to your lives; it can give you strength, strength in all disappointments and grief and pain and feelings of helplessness and misfortune. For you know that at that point you are at the heart of things, you are involved with the real purpose, the meaning of your life. Or better, you are concerned with the one for whom you exist and for whom you are meant.

I once read of an old sick Negro who one evening in church uttered this simple prayer: 'O Lord, thank you for today, a day the like of which we have never seen before.'

You can easily forget to pray, neglect prayer if you pray by yourself. That is why it is a good thing to pray together at fixed times; that is why it is a good thing to have a weekly celebration like these, through which we support and encourage one another.

Finally, something about that child and the wise priest. Of course you've been thinking, 'Oh, that will be the story about the great Augustine again!' This learned bishop was walking on the sea-shore, meditating on God, when he saw a boy busy bringing water from the sea to a hole he had made in the sand. 'You can't get all that water from the sea into your bucket,' he said to the boy. ' Who are you to talk,' he replied, 'trying to get the great God into your tiny head…' But I'm thinking of another child, in a catechism lesson. The priest was talking about dying. A boy put up his hand and anxiously asked a question. Mightn't death be like being born? How? Well, before birth the child receives everything through the mother and gets it all from her; it lives and moves in this mother but it cannot see the mother herself. Only after the shock of birth can the child see its mother. In this life we are wholly surrounded by God, we get everything from him, but we cannot see him. That can happen only after the shock of death. This story made me think of a line in a letter of John which says that now we are already children of God but only later shall we be completely like him because we shall see him as he is.

Now we live in faith, without sight, so I suggest that together we begin to sing the ancient creed which is also an expression of our trust and our hope.

NB The quotation is from Acts 17.27-28. God's longing for us to say 'Father' is in Jeremiah 3.19. Jesus says in Luke 15 that God is happy when we return to him. Remember that the expressions 'in heaven' in v.7 and 'among the angels of God' in v.10 are two of the usual paraphrases for the person of God himself. See also I John 3.2.

The woman taken in adultery: she only just got into the Bible

As I've already said, the Roman Missal is used in our monastery chapel. So the celebrant on Sunday is tied to the passage from the Gospel which is appointed in the Missal for that day. On the last Sunday before Holy Week it was the story of Jesus and the woman taken in adultery, that splendid story which has found a place in chapter 8 of the Gospel of John. First I shall give the text of the Gospel, then my sermon, punctuated by some verses from a psalm, and then I shall describe what was said when some of those present wanted to ask me more questions after the service.

> Early in the morning Jesus went again to the temple; all the people came to him, and he sat down and taught them. The scribes and the Pharisees brought a woman who had been caught in adultery, and placing her in the midst they said to him, 'Teacher, this woman has been caught in the act of adultery. Now in the law Moses commanded us to stone such.' Jesus bent down and wrote with his finger on the ground. And as they continued to ask him, he stood up and said to them, 'Let him who is without sin among you be the first to throw a stone at her.' And once more he bent down and wrote with his finger on the ground. But when they heard it, they went away, one by one, beginning with the eldest, and Jesus was left alone with the woman standing before him. Jesus looked up and said to her, 'Woman, where are they? Has no one condemned you?' She said, 'No one, Lord.' And Jesus said, 'Neither do I condemn you; go, and do not sin again.'

What a marvellous story! You can see it all happening: the people who were listening to Jesus imperceptibly vanish into the background when the scribes appear with the woman they have caught. The accusers form a closed group. The certainty which binds them together comes from outside: they all know the law, and the woman has been caught breaking the law. The saying of Jesus about the first stone throws each of them back on himself. The group solidarity disintegrates. They go off, one

168

by one, while Jesus again begins to write on the ground. They need not feel his gaze on their backs as they depart. Jesus shows the same respect to the person of the woman. He makes her feel that her accusers have gone away. And with a mysterious certainty he sets aside the condemnation that God himself has spoken over her in his law. He pronounces forgiveness on her, a clean sheet, a new beginning to life.

It's a gem of a story about Jesus. Precisely for that reason it is so alien that it has only got into the Gospel by the skin of its teeth. Of course it's in all our printed Bibles. But before the art of printing was invented, Bibles were mass-produced by being copied. Thousands of old manuscripts of the Gospels have been preserved. The funny thing is that in by far the majority of these manuscripts this story about Jesus does not appear. And in the few in which it does appear it sometimes stands in chapter 8 of the Gospel of John and sometimes earlier, either in chapter 7, or right at the end of the Gospel, attached to the conclusion. We also find it inserted in the Gospel of Luke, in chapter 21, just before the passion narrative. So it's an erratic block which only just found a place. We have no idea which evangelist it came from. At all events, it must have been around in the Christian community when the four Gospels were already in circulation.

Although we do not know where it has come from, we can well imagine how the story functioned. At this first period entering a Christian community of Christ was an enormous wrench. You broke with the generally accepted 'Gentile' lifestyle, all those practices which were taken for granted in the world of the time. As they said, you put aside the old man with its desires and sins and you put on Christ. You modelled your life on love, joy, peace, moderation, self-control. So this was a total break with all that was sinful, everything that disrupted your relationships with your real self, with God and with your fellow human beings. A Christian group had to shine in the midst of a crooked and perverse generation. You will recognize all these phrases from the letters of the apostles. Any Christian who committed a serious sin – idolatry, murder or sexual misconduct – thus excluded himself from the infinite salvation in which he or she had obtained a share. After such a lapse, anyone who had seen the light and had tasted the heavenly gifts, who had become a participant in the Holy Spirit, who had already experienced the powers of the world to come, could no longer be saved, and had forfeited his or her chance for good. That is roughly what the author of the letter to the Hebrews says. That is evidently what people felt and proclaimed and practised in this earliest period.

However, as the years went by, increasing numbers of people entered the church. They all wanted to make the break with the Gentile world, to put off the old man, and they all made this promise when they were baptized. But not everyone succeeded in keeping their promises. So a problem arose for a great many church leaders: did they have to exclude for good someone who had been weak and had committed a serious sin? That is what Paul had done in Corinth, applying a slogan from the Old Testament: 'Cast the evildoer from your midst.' Some church leaders certainly felt that way. People had to keep to the apostolic rules. Others argued for gentleness, mercy, forgiveness, for a new chance for Christians who repented of their sins. Confusion about this must have been great, as must have been the despair of Christians who were faced with strict church leaders.

Perhaps it was in these circumstances that a highly gifted and esteemed Christian appeared with that story about Jesus and the woman taken in adultery, and that this story made an immediate impact. One reason for supposing this is that we find the first reference to it in ancient Christian literature in a plea to take penitent sinners back into the church. The so-called *Didascalia*, a kind of church order written shortly after 200 by an authoritative figure, says this to church leaders: 'If you are unmerciful and will not receive the penitent sinner into the church, then you sin against God the Lord, and you have not allowed yourselves to be convinced by what our Lord and Saviour did towards the woman who had sinned. The elders put her before him, left him to judge her and went away. And he said to her, "Go home, neither do I condemn you."'

At that time, here and there, Christians must have said, 'Yes, that story is part of the Gospel, an authentic part,' and then they will have asked copyists to find a place for it in the most revered Gospel, that of John, or in the Gospel of Luke, who lays such great stress on forgiveness. For here, they said, we recognize the Jesus of the old texts. He cared for publicans and sinners, for all those who had been written off by pious Jews and who had even begun to think of themselves in the same terms: we are worthless, there is no good in us, we are evil men. Jesus made them feel that they were worth something, that's clear, and so he opened up to them a way to true repentance after true conversion.

That's also the case among us men and women. If you've hurt someone you can say, 'Yes, I too am a scoundrel, a rotter, I'm just the same.' But that's not true repentance. You can only offer that if you know that the other person loves you, indeed wholly accepts you and does not find you a scoundrel and a rotter. Only then can you honestly confess what you did wrong and show true repentance. Only then is there a basis for true penitence, for forgiveness and a new life.

We shall now sing a verse from Psalm 51, praying for forgiveness in the certainty that we may ask this because God loves us.

The scribes and the Pharisees departed one by one. Jesus had touched the conscience of each one of them, and this destroyed the certainty that bound them together. But if you think about the sequel of the story, you can imagine how they found each other in a new certainty; they will have said to themselves: 'This can't be right, this man is undermining the law and morality.'

This picture, too, would agree with the earliest texts in the Gospels. It is certain that Jesus concern' for sinners was what brought him to the cross. He had to be done away with because he shocked the religious world with his God who loves everybody and wants everybody to have a sense of being loved and therefore being able to love. It was his deepest conviction, the basis of his life, that man is really made for love and achieves fulfilment through loving.

Because of this message and this experience, Jesus was done away with. He accepted his death to convince us of this divine love and to involve us in it. That is why we proclaim this death of the Lord as long as the world lasts, until he comes, every time we celebrate the eucharist. In it he gives us himself in bread and wine, a sign that he accepts us in love, us, together, so that we accept one another in love and on that basis continually forgive one another.

It is an inexhaustible mystery, the fact of this man Jesus among us, living from God for us, God with us. The best we can do is to sing about it, though even then the words fall short. For the text of the hymn contains the line 'In everything like us'. Is that really true? Isn't the special thing about this man that he lived completely in and from God's love and could make it flow down unimpeded upon people? So he spoke and acted on the basis of a great inner certainty and repose. The narrator of our story also gives us a splendid indication of this. Jesus could sit writing on the ground, and he could penetrate the hearts of the accusers and thus confidently offer the woman a new beginning, a fresh start. May God grant that we may be made a bit more like him every day, beginning today.

Discussion afterwards

At the end of the celebration some churchgoers wanted to talk a bit more. When I asked what about, a few came up with questions about the historical truth of the Gospel story. A lawyer in my group had some doubts over what Jesus said about casting the first stone, that this could be done only by those who were themselves without sin. In that case no judge could possibly pronounce sentence. Moreover, he felt, even then marriage had to be protected by legislation. If a society passes over such far-reaching actions as adultery as lightly as Jesus does here, then it destroys itself. 'But apart from that,' he added, 'if I remember rightly, Jesus was very strict on the question of marital faithfulness. A man who looks at another man's wife covetously has already committed adultery with her in his heart. I think he says that in the Sermon on the Mount.'

What I had said about the opposition between Christian communities and the wicked pagan world outside had evoked a protest from one of the women, the mother of grown-up and nearly grown-up children. There were also good people in that Gentile world, she said. Once again I heard the argument that Christianity could be very irritating to young people in particular, with its argument that good can only be found among Christians.

When it came to the question of historical truth I replied that according to most interpreters the story is not historical in the sense of being an eyewitness account, a newspaper report, or even a clear reminiscence. We could call it historical in the sense that it gives us a characteristic portrait of the historical Jesus. I had emphasized this last point in my sermon. Of course I couldn't say anything in church about the first point, its unhistorical character. Even had there been time for a longer sermon, that sort of thing is inappropriate in a context in which no conversation and no discussion is possible. But in this conversation I could produce some of the reasons why the story does not look like a factual account. It is very different from what the first three Gospels say about Jesus' ministry. That he should have intervened in a legal case and prevented sentence being passed goes against what they say. In the first three Gospels, the only woman to whom Jesus promises forgiveness for her sins is the so-called woman who was a sinner in the moving story in Luke 7. Evidently she has already experienced forgiveness, or rather the certainty of being accepted by God and shows this to Jesus who is reclining at table, openly expressing her gratitude by washing his feet with her tears and then anointing them and kissing them passionately. She is clearly a prostitute, a whore, not a married woman taken in adultery.

Our narrator envisages the circumstances of Jesus' time much less aptly than the first three evangelists. He supposes that any given group of scribes and Pharisees at that time had the right to carry out a death sentence. That is something that even the highest instrument of government in the Jewish community, the Sanhedrin, could not do – at all events, not without the approval of the Roman authorities. Or were they about to lynch the woman? And did they have to ask Jesus' advice? The reason which some manuscripts add, namely that they came to Jesus to put him to the test and so find reason to accuse him, seems to have been borrowed from the old Gospel stories. In them the Pharisees and Scribes often try to catch Jesus out.

The narrator also does not think of what will happen to the woman in the Jewish society of her time after Jesus has released her. Is her lawful husband to take her back? There is no mention of repentance on her side, nor even of good intentions.

It seems to me that the narrator is concerned with the two sayings which he puts in the mouth of Jesus and which he intends for the Christian community. In that community no one is to pass judgment on anyone else. And everyone must always be ready to forgive, no matter what wrong has been done to him or her. For the members have been called to be a community which already experiences something of what Jesus called the kingdom of God. That is a kind of society which is governed by everyone's concern for God, the God whom Jesus addressed as Abba, Father. Do not condemn, he said vigorously, and he added the vivid comparison of the splinter in one man's eye and the beam in the other's. Jesus also says that you cannot have a relationship with the Father unless you are prepared to forgive what others do to you, and are prepared to do so unconditionally. It seems clear to me that our storyteller made these ideals of Jesus entirely his own and that at the same time he was also very strongly attracted by the mystery of Jesus' bond with God, who gave him such unprecedented inward calm and thus a clear view of what moves people most deeply.

As I have already said, the members of such a Christian community felt themselves to be called together by God; by him they had been taken out to the realm of darkness and brought into the kingdom of his beloved Son, to use words from the letter to the Colossians. I could quote a great many more stories in which the enthusiasm and the gratitude of the first generations of Christians shine through, and their joy at being brought together in this way, 'saved', as they often say, from a society which from their point of view could only be regarded as being corrupt through and through. In their eyes this corruption chiefly derived from the all-pervading worship of the many gods and goddesses and the immoral practices which went with it, especially in the sexual sphere. Of course, modern scholars familiar with the society of the time present a much more sophisticated picture. In their view there were always people who could be described with words which Paul uses in his letter to the Philippians, concerned for 'all that is true, all that is noble, all that is just and pure, all that is lovable and gracious, whatever is excellent and admirable'. But the Christians strove for all these human values as a group incorporated into Jesus, the Messiah or Christ, whom they sometimes called the new man, the new Adam. In other words, they did this corporately in such a way that all forms of mutual discrimination were at an end among them. They were all addressed as human beings. It was precisely this special way of dealing with one another, this mutual love, which was the attraction of this new movement, above all in the great cities of the empire. With the arrival of so many new members the problem also arose which I touched on in my sermon: what was the attitude to be to Christians who lapsed into one of the major sins, like idolatry, murder or adultery.

New problems arose much later, when the Christians were no longer a small minority in the Roman empire, unconcerned with the life of society. At that time Christians held responsible public offices. Some were judges, others held posts in the army. Then the radical demands of Jesus caused a great many problems. As a judge you had to pronounce sentences although you knew that you yourself were not without sin. As a soldier you had to use force, and you were involved in killing fellow human beings.

Postscript

After a celebration in our chapel on Easter Eve, a young woman came up to me. She was obviously rather offended. 'Luke,' she said, 'that's not my God.' She had got to know me in a Bible group for students. Now she was in an advanced state of pregnancy with her first child. 'What do you mean, Agnes?' 'Well,' she said, 'Why did he have to kill the firstborn children of the Egyptian slaves as well? Liberator from slavery, they say so calmly.'

During the service the reading had been a kind of collage of texts from the book of Exodus. The texts had been chosen in such a way as to bring out the liberating character of the event much more strongly than if we had had the long biblical narrative. It had made a deep impression on me. But Agnes had got stuck with one passage: 'Yahweh said: At midnight I shall go round Egypt. Every firstborn in Egypt shall die, from the firstborn of Pharaoh who shall succeed him to the firstborn of the slaves who turn the mill.'

That had made her cross. I was also a bit cross when I replied that these texts were not concerned with facts. She should have remembered that from her evenings of Bible study! It is a story of faith. Israel believed in her God as saviour and redeemer, and on the basis of that faith the story of the Exodus grew longer and more powerful. It developed into a liturgical hymn of praise, a kind of epic. The telling of it, with increasing excitement, was at the same time a means of strengthening that faith in new times of need. Pharaoh and Egypt become symbols of all the powers of disaster which were to threaten Israel.

But in that case what do you make of the killing of all the firstborn? I would suggest something like this. Israel experienced its bond with Yahweh as a relationship which it sometimes compared to a father-son relationship. You find that expressed for the first time in Hosea 11, which contains the famous sentence, 'Out of Egypt have I called my son.' In that case this detail in the epic of the Exodus comes from that imagery: Yahweh commands the Pharaoh to let his son depart from Egypt; if Pharaoh does not do this, Yahweh will kill his firstborn son. In the epic, that develops into becoming the death of all the firstborn in Egypt, from high to low, from the Pharaoh to the slaves. That's what happens in this kind of story. Don't forget that among people of antiquity the firstfruits of the field, the first offspring of the cattle and the firstborn of men and women had a religious significance: this was the way in which the deity showed that he was prepared to go on giving life. To say that all the firstborn of Egypt were affected was the same as saying that the powers which threatened Israel were robbed of their living force, their future, that they could do nothing more in the face of the liberating power of Yahweh. In other words, I told Agnes, as I have often said, here too we have belief in story form. And the story was told and sung on our Easter Eve as an expression of our belief in the saving God who in Jesus had robbed even the threatening power of death of its force.

Agnes nodded thoughtfully. As she went away I promised her that I would return to the matter again. Not when I first came to see the baby! But I didn't feel very satisfied with my explanation. It is easy to say something of this kind when you yourself don't feel a child growing your belly! But above all, my explanation wasn't complete. This Yahweh in whom Israel believed wasn't just hard on Egypt. I thought of texts from the book of Deuteronomy, e.g. chapter 7, which says through Moses something like this: as Yahweh acted against Egypt, so too he will act against the people who live in the promised land; moreover, he will annihilate them and root them out. Our modern translations tend to use the words 'drive out': he will drive out these people from before Israel, chase them away. But the oldest translations usually express the precise meaning of the Hebrew verb: annihilate. Yahweh annihilates these peoples so that they no longer exist, no longer have claims, and then he assigns their land to his own people. In some texts it is Yawheh himself who annihilates them, and in others that happens at his command through Moses, Joshua, or particular tribes.

This theme occurs often in the history books which were edited by the 'Deuteronomists'. As I said in chapter 2 (pp.12-16 above) these reformers had been struck by the disasters which had affected first Israel and then Judah. They completed their work in exile, when the land which had once been promised was lost. Why had Yahweh brought these disasters upon his people. The answer was: under the leadership of their kings they had taken over gods and religious customs from other peoples, above all from the Canaanites. If they wanted to be the true people of Yahweh, from then on they should have wiped out all traces of that paganism from their midst; anything that was in the least bit Canaanite had to be rooted out mercilessly. Only then would Yahweh again allow them into the land which he had given to their fathers. These reformers expressed this conviction in their stories about the first arrival of Israel in that promised land. In the footsteps of Moses, Joshua and others had carried out Yahweh's will to annihilate the pagan peoples there completely. So this was a proclamation of faith in the form of stories about the distant past.

These were not entirely the fruit of the imagination of believers. In the centuries during which the tribes of Israel gained a firm footing in Canaan, and sometimes in later periods, people would sacrifice the whole population of a conquered city in honour of their own deity; this was a real 'holocaust'. That was a custom of the people in this area, and Israel was no exception. But the stories in which this practice is applied wholesale, in accordance with Yahweh's intentions, are comparable with the epic of the Exodus.

The Jews who returned from Babylonia in the years after 538 had no military or political power. They formed a religious community under the leadership of priests, a kind of 'church'. Round about the year 400 the reformers Ezra and Nehemiah came to put the finishing touches to its way of life. In the biblical books named after them (Ezra 9 and 10; Nehemiah 13) we can read about the measures they took to purify the community: Jewish men who were married to non-Jewish wives had to put away their spouses and their children. Here we can detect the religous zeal of the Deuteronomists, solemn and inexorably harsh and inhuman to non-Jews.

I wanted to talk with Agnes a bit more about this aspect of

Yahweh. The opportunity for that arose unexpectedly. Her baby was already some months old when we next met – not counting my visit after the baby's birth – and it was again after a church service.

On a Sunday in Peace Week a woman from Jerusalem was speaking in the student church, one of four Palestinian Christians who had been invited to Holland in order to discuss their situation with fellow Christians. Her address during the service had made a great impression. There was not a trace of anger or hatred against the occupying forces. The one thing she did express in strong terms in the name of her people was the desire to be looked on and treated as human beings, on the same footing as the Israeli Jews. She also read a poem by a famous Palestinian poetess in Arabic, after we had first heard a Dutch translation. The whole church listened to these Arabic sounds with bated breath.

I stayed behind to talk to a few people, including Agnes. The question arose whether there are also religious motives behind the harsh measures against the Palestinian population and the increasing confiscation of their property. Or is it purely a political matter, that is to say a question of the future of the nation and national security? Most of us suppose that there are religious motives. I certainly do, though I think that they tend to be inextricably interwoven with political and strategic considerations. It is well known that the biblical book of Joshua plays a major part in the education of young people and also in military training. Here the stories about Joshua's onslaught on the population of Canaan are regarded as historical accounts. An investigation in various schools at the beginning of the 1960s showed what most children took for granted: what Joshua then did to the inhabitants of the promised land their army could not do to the Palestinians.

I immediately thought of a remark Golda Meir continued to make for years: Palestinians do not exist; there are no such things. This made me think of the term 'annihilate', which occurs so often in the Hebrew text. Menachim Begin, who was then her minister, once explained the official statement in this way: If Palestinians exist, we have deprived a people of its land and in that case we have no right to live here!

And so we arrived at the theme which had made Agnes so

179

cross on Easter Eve: is not this Yahweh inhuman, at least to those who do not belong to his people? A psychologist went into this at great length. He used technical terms like 'narcissistic' and 'archetypes' with which I am not familiar. But what he meant was clear to me and the others. According to him, the Jews had created a very powerful God because they had a weak sense of themselves. They felt threatened by the peoples of Canaan and neighbouring countries, so these people had to disappear. Their own powerful God would see to that. This is a very human pattern. Because of its own helplessness, a child needs a completely omnipotent father. If its own father seems to be not so powerful, a god is put in his place. 'That's Freud!' someone interrupted. He didn't explain further, but just said that every belief can gain authenticity when this kind of human pattern, this kind of psychological mechanism, is recognized.

The pressure because of your own weakness to make someone or something into an archetype, an entity on which everything, your whole existence, depends, is a very human one, but it also leads to inhumanities: *the* great leader, *the* hero, *the* woman, and also *the* revelation, *the* holy book. To my delight the man pointed out how Jesus reacted to the tendency of people to begin to revere him in this way. 'Me, good? Come now! Me a judge in your concerns? No, look after that yourselves.' I was surprised by what the psychiatrist said about the women who came to mourn with Jesus on his way to the cross, as the evangelist Luke describes them. Such lamentation went with the cult of the Egyptian deity Osiris, a dying and rising god. Jesus wanted nothing to do with such veneration. 'Weep for yourselves,' he said soberly. Thus in the gospel there is criticism of this basic human tendency to create archetypes.

And so we came to dealing with the Bible. The revelation of God? I recalled the beginning of Isaiah 63. There Yahweh is poetically described as a man who comes from Edom, where he has trampled the whole population as a vine-grower treads his grapes. Yahweh's garments are stained with blood. The Edomites had collaborated with the Babylonians when they devastated Jerusalem in 587 and had reaped the benefits. Hence the Jewish hatred of them and hence this picture of Yahweh. The revelation of God? Or the revelation of the understandable feelings of vengeance on the part of the victims? The 'prophetic' books have

180

whole sections full of divine sayings against neighbouring peoples, whose destruction is usually announced. Of course there are also sayings in which we are told that Yahweh also wants to bring other nations to himself, like Egypt and Assyria in the sublime conclusion to Isaiah 19, or the whole world of the Gentiles in the story of Jonah.

So do you choose these texts, the 'humane' texts which suit you, and leave the others aside? We began to discuss how we dealt with the Bible in connection with such problems. It's a question of really coming to terms with it, entering into dialogue with the people who express their beliefs and their ideas in the Bible. We are quite free to say to them, 'Look, at this point aren't you projecting your own feelings, perhaps of revenge?' Or, 'Aren't you giving divine approval to certain patterns of life?' I brought out this last point when we were talking about the role of women. When we read in Paul's letters, 'Women, be subservient to men,' we are entitled to object. 'Sorry Paul, we're in process of developing different patterns. We always listen to you with gratitude when you are telling us how you were affected by Christ and live by your relationship with him, dedicate your life to human happiness. You have written about the mystery of God and the working of the Spirit in texts which we know inside out because they keep prodding us. But when you talk about the status of women in family and society you're thinking in patterns which are no longer ours, and then we part company with you.'

I wanted to end this book with a few extracts from the discussion with Agnes and with this group. Someone thought I was 'liberal' in the way I dealt with the Bible. Yes, that's deliberate. I recently ended an article in a journal for monks and nuns with a quotation from Henriette Kraemer, well known for her work in organizing aid projects in developing countries. In an interview in the journal *Bijeen* she gave this advice. 'Note carefully the significance of liberal Jews in Israel, like the liberal Christians in Lebanon and the liberal Moslems in various countries.' It is the liberals who detach themselves from the fanatical elements in their religion and become open to humanity.

I ended by saying that I myself would want all Christians to deal in a very liberal way with the Bible and its themes, using this liberality, this freedom which is given to us in Christ: we have the freedom to judge biblical texts and the way in which they are used by the clear norm which Jesus himself has given us, and which God has acknowledged to be his by raising him from the dead.